PRAISE FOR
DOCTORING THE DEVIL

"What some call superstition you will see in *Doctoring the Devil* is a way of life for the folks of the Appalachian Mountains. I love the stories Jake tells here and the weaving of the tales. Jake has outdone himself! He always seems to place hidden gems within his writings."
—STARR CASAS, author of *Old Style Conjure* and *Divination Conjure Style*

"I do believe Jake has outdone himself. There are so many gems in *Doctoring the Devil* that should be read more than once. I personally love the explanations given here as well as the proper distinctions between certain works. The clouds in the sky definitely speak a message, as he so eloquently writes. This is a wonderful read—full of instructional jewels. You will be blessed by the words given here and the wisdom that lines this book's pages."
—HOODOO SEN MOISE, author of *Working Conjure: A Guide to Hoodoo Folk Magic*

DOCTORING the DEVIL

DOCTORING the DEVIL

Notebooks of an Appalachian Conjure Man

JAKE RICHARDS

WEISER BOOKS

This edition first published in 2021 by Weiser Books, an imprint of
Red Wheel/Weiser, LLC
With offices at:
65 Parker Street, Suite 7
Newburyport, MA 01950
www.redwheelweiser.com

Bible verses in the text are from the King James edition.

ISBN: 978-1-57863-733-1
Library of Congress Cataloging-in-Publication Data available upon request.

Cover design by Kathryn Sky-Peck
Moth art © Xunbin Pan/Dreamstime
Interior by Maureen Forys, Happenstance Type-O-Rama
Typeset in Adobe Jenson Pro, Hey Thalissa and Alligator

Printed in the United States of America
IBI
10 9 8 7 6 5 4 3 2 1

To my grandmother, Mrs. Margaret Trivett,
March 1939–January 2020

*The mountains shall bring peace to the people,
and the little hills, by righteousness.*

PSALM 72:3

CONTENTS

ACKNOWLEDGMENTS

None of this work, nor this writing, would have been possible without the aid of my ancestors. Writing demands sacrifices, not only of time and energy, but also of faith and love. Like many things that are spirit led, you walk into it blindly, without a clue as to how it will turn out. Much like writing, life is the same.

Each time I write, life has its demands and the enemy throws everything he can at me to stop me. With each writing, my family has endured hard times and trials, from strokes and blood clots to my grandmother's hip surgery during the writing of this book.

Mrs. Margaret was born in March 1939 to wonderful parents. She went to church her whole life and knew who she was and what she wanted to be. She played piano in grade school and had a talent for it—she could replicate any tune she heard just by listening. She worked as a certified nurse for most of her life until she retired, all the while making and raising a family with my grandfather, Gene. They met in church and he showed up on her porch one day and asked her out. They got married in 1958. Together they raised not only their own family but also hundreds of foster children who needed a home filled with love. At Nana's house there was plenty of that. You never left without being fed or cared for in some way.

From a very young age, she was my best friend. It may sound cliché to say I always sat at her feet to hear stories and talk with her up until she passed, but it's true. We always sat at the foot of her recliner to listen to her and enjoy her company. But life goes on, and we grow up and opportunities take us away from home. But every chance I got I was hearing her stories.

After Papaw passed, she started showing signs of dementia. It's the hardest thing to watch someone you love disappear a little bit each day, all while seeing them and holding their hand. We figure God gave it to her because He knew she wouldn't be able to handle the heartbreak of losing Papaw after forty-seven years of marriage.

Even with the dementia, though, and her memory coming and going, she was always herself—maybe herself before she had kids or before she had grandkids, but she always knew herself. It was like simultaneously losing her, but meeting who she was at different points in her life. Regardless of what happened, she was always wrapped in dignity and peace. We made sure she stayed that way to the end.

She was a strong woman in the flesh but even more so in the spirit. In the days leading up to her passing, my mother (who has the sight) continuously saw her surrounded by her mama and daddy and her lost love; heard angels singing as the windows shook; and saw the light hands of ancestors reaching to comfort her from the picture frames on the wall. I was sure the world would end when she went, but I told her we'd be fine. That morning, as we waited for the coroner to come, the sun broke through the clouds after a long week of rain and it was the most beautiful, colorful morning I'll ever live to see. After that the world lost some color, but the Land of Beulah gained it.

We weren't sure how we would go about the funeral. We didn't have the money or the insurance for it. I was willing to do anything to make sure that wonderful saint of a woman was laid to rest with the dignity she lived by and not in pinewood box. We spoke with bank after bank; we tried every possible thing we could do until a friend made a fund for it once I put aside my pride. To my surprise and amazement, we were able to raise the funds for her burial, all donated by past clients I've helped. It still has me speechless, and I can never repay any of you for that blessing.

So, Nana, I hope you can somehow see this book like you did the first. I hope you know I will never forget you. That's why I'm saying this here. Because a saint died on Exum Street and the world kept going on without you. So here in this moment, on this page, you're still with me. And we can remember, together.

DOCTORING the DEVIL

INTRODUCTION

I have lived in east Tennessee my whole life, but I've also traveled across the country—and I swear there ain't no better place than Appalachia. Maybe I'm biased, but after seeing the rest of the country, I understand what Nana meant when she said this was God's country. Appalachia, the "never-ending forest," continues to surprise me. The growth of culture, both animal and human, is astounding, as is the relationship between the two connected by blood and spirit, sometimes quite literally. I've worked roots and conjure now going on thirteen years, having learned from my elders, from my dreams, and from my own experience. I was raised by family in many places—my mother's home, her mama's house going toward Piney Flats, Tennessee, my paternal great-grandfather's in Unicoi, Tennessee, and my paternal great-grandmother's holler in North Carolina, near Devil's Nest on Big Ridge. I'd play in corn rows, catch caterpillars in a jar. In the spring, I'd be chest-deep in the mountain creek beneath the little bridge covered in wild yellow roses, opening my chest from the previous winter. From an early age, I was exposed to the local lore in each community, equipped with stories that would one day be of aid one way or another.

When I was young, I helped in the gardens and barns, picking pears and gathering chicken eggs and sometimes duck eggs from the pond. Just about everyone here did, growing up. I'd watch intently as my grandmothers canned the beans and tomatoes, cracking the whip of country wisdom and making something almost eternal, like scientists in a lab. God strike me if I'm lying, but I'll bet you anything they've still got some of those jars that six-year-old me watched them can!

I grew up being told to get "warshed" up for dinner, to get a mint from Nana's "poke" bag during church while Papaw preached. I was raised on porch swings, old men trading news over a coffee or beer, wives and sisters standing outside talking on warm summer nights until the wee hours of the morning. My alarm clock was the morning sun and the occasional rooster; my lullaby was often the howls of coyotes while fireflies carried stars down from heaven.

I have always had a wonderful relationship with animals—I think everyone from here does. However, I think I was almost to the point of giving Mama a heart attack. I'd wander off and play beneath a bull in a cow field, or tangle with a copperhead my daddy caught in a minnow trap. Mama said I had snake charmer's blood, meaning a person who isn't easily bit by snakes because of some charm naturally cast by the holder. We were around wild animals every day, and we respected them and they respected us. This added to my relationship with the land as nature, and its inhabitants became not only a window into God, but also a window into myself, reflecting back to me the good and the bad, like water pooling in the still eddies off the creek. Animals and plants play a very large role in the way we're born, live, cook, clean, work, and die, so of course they have a role in Appalachian folk magic and the work of a hilltop conjure man.

We grew up on stories of witches and family encounters with the Devil; stories of local spirits and creatures that roam the hills. My grandfather was a faith healer who had the sight. He cured thrush and warts, stopped blood with a prayer, and stole a fever with an egg. His mama may have also done this work. I never met Mamaw Seagle, but my mother has told me stories of her home on Pine Street in Johnson City, Tennessee, that the walls seemed like they were breathing, and there would be cold spots in the dead of summer even though Mamaw didn't have an air conditioner. Mama said she always had oil lamps going and something burning with a musky smell on the stove.

She loved the woman to death, but she hated going to her home. My maternal great-grandmother, Sadie Mae, from the melungeon[1] side of my mother's family, used to make dolls and hide them for some reason. Her husband, a white man, we think was a conjure man also due to a photo we found of him posing with a doll that has black feathers attached to it.

Mama also has the Gift as a seventh daughter. Her mama has the sight, too; anything she says has passed and will pass. She has always had those weird quirks that everybody notices but doesn't put much thought into. I think she enjoyed it until I came along! See, I was born "blue," which is said to be an indicator of the Gift or the sight in Appalachia. Being born breech, sunny-side up (that is, faceup instead of facedown), or with a veil over the eyes (when the baby has part of the amniotic sac covering its head or face) was dangerous for the child, and many died— so it was said that those who survived were extremely lucky, born from the jaws of death, and walk that line until they enter the grave.

When my elders began passing away, I dedicated myself to collecting this lore, and keeping track of the beliefs and tales I heard growing up. Being born blue, I grew up hearing things that weren't said aloud by anyone present, knowing what someone was going to say before they said it or how they were faring, and sensing what was about to happen. My sister, a "left twin," or a surviving twin since our sister died in the womb before birth, also has these gifts. These occurrences, like speaking with the dead openly, laying salt and cinnamon at the doors, or being healed by my mother's hands instead of the doctor, weren't anything strange to us.

---

1 *Melungeon* is a term used for triracial people in east Tennessee. We are mostly thought to be a mixture of European, Portuguese, Native American, and African, often characterized by our dark hair and olive skin. This term likely arises from the French word *mélange*, meaning "mixture." Originally a slur denoting "dirty" or "tainted," it has been reclaimed in recent times.

There have been many books coming forth to help preserve our culture: how we pray, how we cook and eat, what toys our kids play with, how we work and dress, how we birth and bury our own. However, largely kept to the side, out of sight and out of mind, are the secret doings of how we handled when the deck was stacked against us: those secrets kept in the home, or those secret ventures to meet that one person everybody was wary of. Folk magic and conjure have played a big role in Appalachian life for centuries, being a mix of cultural beliefs from the native tribes such as the Cherokee and the immigrant people who settled here: Germans, English, and Scotts-Irish. And it's high time that folks knew it and quit throwing it off as simple old wives' tales. Back in the day, these folks weren't talked about much, let alone written about, so many of the stories that have remained are oral stories passed around. That is the reason for my writing: to help preserve these traditions and, in a way, to revive that culture of superstition and tales that is unique to southern Appalachia. First we will meet some of the key figures in Appalachian folk magic, understand them and the tales that remain. Then it's off to the top of the mountain to meet the roots of money, love, and justice and see how they are worked.

1

WITCHCRAFT AND CONJURE IN APPALACHIA

Every man was his own doctor and priest back in the day, until as recently as the early to mid-twentieth century, when Western medicine and stationary preachers became more abundant. Before that, every family or community had usually one to three people who helped with a range of ailments, from bleeding and infections to nightmares and supposed curses. These same folks would also deliver babies, perform baptisms, marry couples, and bury the deceased. Now the folks who did this were as varied as their titles, but the most fascinating character in the hills was the root person. This was the old woman who knew everything whispered in the dark, and the man who came over the hills to cure you of a curse, holding a bucket of vomited crickets and salamanders.

God listens to our prayers and knows what we need. But we Appalachian Americans have a certain self-reliance. We were left to fend for ourselves for the longest time while simultaneously being robbed of resources by outsiders, whether it was coal or timber or what have you. There wasn't anything else here they wanted or cared for to the point some transport trains didn't even stop here for anything but to fuel up. Therefore there was rarely a train that came through with news of the outside world or anything like that. Otherwise it was us and

God. We didn't have preachers or priests down the road to pray for us—we prayed for each other. The preachers we did have were circuit riders who traveled from community to community constantly, maybe staying in one place for a week to preach, baptize, or bless. Otherwise, it was just us, fending for ourselves, growing our own food and making our own work.

Because we were all taught that God only gives you what you can handle, we will try everything to make ends meet before giving up and giving it to God. And a good first step before seeking His help is to find the conjurer or root person of the community. These healers had a way about them, a way of seeing and walking, that allowed them to speak with the spirits to bring about change. The way it was taught to me is that everybody's life is like a water pipe: it flows and flows, but sometimes things get clogged up to the point where the water (the person) can't overcome it on their own; so they call up a friend first (root doctor) to see what the issue is and to see if it can be worked quick before calling the plumber (God), who works by their own time. This is what the doctor does; they move things around in your life to create the best and most beneficial flow for you.

TYPES OF WORKERS

There have been many kinds of mystical folks in these hills, each with his or her own title or name for their particular spiritual trade. Some folks stick to just one degree, such as faith healing, while others cross barriers, drawing on several practices or methods. There are many, many names that denote the same type of worker. For our purposes, we will stick with the most common titles and names that most are familiar with.

Faith Healers

Faith healers, also known as high men or power doctors, aid with ailments by the movements of their hands, the ease of their breath, and the power of prayer. The word *power* here may be a corruption of the title used in northern Appalachia: *powwow* being changed to *powower*, and eventually to the current form. Faith healers might also be known as fire talkers, wart charmers, thrush doctors, blood stoppers, and more, which alludes to their specialties.

Root and Yarb Doctors

Root and yarb doctors, also sometimes called remedy men, help people using roots and bark. *Yarb* is a corruption of the word *herb* and was mostly used in the hills and mountains, while *herb doctor* was the term used in the valleys and cities. The folks who cure in this manner were known in their communities as the local doctor, and they often had titles attached to their names.

Oftentimes, for a woman, regardless of age or parenthood, she was called granny, mammy, aunt, or maw before her name, so Mammy Smith or Granny Easle. This was a term of respect and endearment. Men were called doc, doctor, uncle, or paw. In researching my family lineage, I have found a handful of grandfathers and uncles who are named on census records and other documents as doc so-and-so, although there's no record of them being anything but a farmer or other worker. This could be an indication of their possible side profession as a yarb doctor.

Men who were seventh sons, or the seventh son of a seventh son, were also given the nickname "Doc" due to the belief that men born as the seventh son were destined to be healers in some manner. The widely known granny woman, who was usually the midwife, also aided with minor maladies such as cracking feet, cuts or bruises, colic, and the like, but usually didn't perform surgery or bloodletting, or prescribe any "store doctor" drugs such as mercury or Indian vegetable pills, an old-time cure-all that was sold back then for a wide variety of ailments. This was during the time when folks were getting used to pharmacies popping up, and we are sure stubborn creatures of habit, so we never let go of our herbs (that is, until recently, once folks stopped passing down remedies).

Cow and Horse Doctors

There were also doctors who specialized solely in animals and livestock. They often used herbs gathered from the land or liniments and other drugs from the local drugstore prepared in at-home ways to heal animals. These were often simply called cow or horse doctors, although there's little record of this title being added to anyone's name. Both root doctors and cow or horse doctors sometimes also employed practices of Western medicine used at the time, such as bloodletting, cupping, vaccine administration, and even surgery.

Witchdoctors, Conjurers, Root Workers, Hex Doctors, Witch Finders, and Love Doctors

Next, we have the witchdoctor, the conjurer, the root worker, the hex doctor, the witch finder, and the love doctor. The witchdoctor and conjurers, or the root worker (as opposed to root doctor), worked roots not only for medicine of the body but also for the mind and spirit. Horton Cooper calls them "hex doctors," which is a carryover from Germany, where the word *hexen* means "witch." The hex doctor sold powders and roots such as Adam and Eve root (an orchid native to the mountains) and High John the Conqueror root. There were also love doctors, who aided folks in finding and keeping love or calling a lover back home. They gave powders to be sprinkled in the lover's path or directly on them, created the hex or root, and doctored it.

While many know this as conjure or root work, those raised in the work and in the know called it "doctoring the devil," whether you're doctoring a root for someone or doctoring them of a root they're currently under. This title acknowledges how fine the line is between God and the Devil. It's easy to sway with the power.

Folk Magic versus Conjure

Some say anyone can become a true conjurer or witchdoctor, while others say you have to have a gift for it in order to do it right. Here is where I will make the distinction, as I see it, between folk magic and conjure. Folk magic or root work is the magical act of using roots and things to influence, incapacitate, attract, avert, or change a situation of the present or future in some manner. This includes superstitions such as tossing salt over your shoulder, exiting the same door you entered through lest your spirit get trapped, turning your pockets inside out to avert bad luck, and carrying a buckeye or walnut in the pocket for luck or to ease arthritis. These kinds of things are practiced knowingly or out of habit by the majority of folks in Appalachia. Folk magic is any superstitious action taken without an appeal or prayer to a higher spirit or divinity that is alleged to cause a supernatural result. It works by belief, the power of the person with the root, and the power of the action taken. Much of Appalachian folk magic and superstition is based on sympathetic magic where like actions create like causes, such as turning your pockets inside out to also turn inside out or away the bad luck. The power behind these was furthered in our picking them up from the old folks without question. Without question because we see that they work!

Conjure, on the other hand, is the direct and intentional employment of spirits, whether they be spirits of the graveyard, the ancestors, simple spirits of the land you live on, or some other presence, to work on your behalf. This also includes angels and God. Yes, God is worked with here. He is the first conjurer, after all, conjuring up the world in seven days. Conjure is root work and folk magic but with a helping hand, whether it's helping you get a bird's-eye view of a situation or taking care of things for you. Conjurers are experts when it comes to the unseen: they know how to deal with it, make it, handle it, cure it, or repel it. They take folk magic a bit deeper and knowingly work and twist the hand of nature in their favor.

We walk both here and in spirit simultaneously, and sometimes continuously. It's nothing for me to walk down the streets in Old Jonesborough and have a conversation with both the neighborly shop owners as well as the spirits that wander the roads alongside them. Growing up, and still to this day, I'll see my mother and grandmother speak about or to spirits they see. Nana sometimes sees a woman out the window, standing at the crossroads. She'll wave, but she says the woman doesn't wave back. Nana has also seen many people across the street throwing a barbecue, yet no one is physically in the yard.

In Appalachia, among those with the Gift and the sight, the veil between the living and the dead is very thin, sometimes nonexistent. If someone doesn't know what's going on or why they keep seeing things, it can very well drive them mad. Because they're scared, they don't know what's going on, and they can't tell what is physically there and what's not. It can't be controlled, only slipped into like a suit. However, at the beginning the suit can wear you instead of you wearing it!

DEGREES OF PRACTICE

I'm going to explain the difference between each degree of practitioners here, but be mindful they often cross and intersect a lot, examples of which we will see later. So there may be some faith healers who are also yarb or root doctors. There may be some root doctors who are also root workers, using roots to aid not only the body but also the mind and soul. Furthermore, anyone could be a little bit of all: a faith healer who uses roots to heal and to bring money, love, or justice. Then they may stay separate altogether, based on upbringing and personal belief. I've met some faith healers who'll have nothing to do with working roots because they believe that it's evil or that they can't handle the power. There are also tales of yarb doctors disbelieving that roots can draw money or that you can conjure the dead or other spirits. So this isn't a set area, but an array of beliefs and degrees of practice separated only by the hills of our ancestors.

Taking into account the actions and practices by the other working folks prior, there's a bit of both folk magic and conjure done by each, whether some are aware of it or not. The degrees of faith healing, root doctoring, and conjuring often overlap. The faith healers pray to the angels and to God to aid in healing using Bible verses, so naturally it includes a certain degree of conjuring, not only in the aspect of calling on spiritual aid but also in hand movements or superstitious practices as well, such as my grandfather using an egg to take out a fever by passing the egg over the head a certain way with prayers; he was not only praying to God for relief, his hands were working in the relief by conjuring the fever out and into a more suitable home that can take its heat: the egg.

Sometimes the healer would give the person restrictions on diet or activities based on superstitious belief. For example, for swellings it would be recommended to abstain from fish or anything caught from the water until the third Sunday after the swelling had subsided. In the case of burns, once the "fire" was gone, you had to wait for that window to close, a window in which the "fire" could hop back into the burn. This is why folklore often recommends refraining from lighting fires or using matches and lighters until after a burn has healed. If a burn is allowed to fester with the "fire" still in it, it will reach the bone and cause a scar. But those able to reach a burn doctor in time often had complete recovery with no scarring, regardless of the severity of the burn.

Preachers also sometimes resort to divination to speak with God and the spirits through bibliomancy: opening the Bible to a random page and verse after a question or need has been stated to find the answer or solution on said page. Nana and Papaw did this and said if you ask a question and open the Bible to a verse where Christ is speaking, or to a verse that begins "and it came to pass," then that is a strong yes to your question.

The yarb or root doctor healed with herbs and usually didn't stick with the simple physical medicine of pills and herb, and these were numerous throughout the region. Just about anyone could pick up a copy of *Gunn's Domestic Medicine*, get a horse, a bag, a lancet, and a few drugs and other tools and call himself a doctor or physician. John C. Gunn specifically wrote his book for these folks. In the event that a "trained" physician couldn't be reached, it taught you what to do until such a time. Because the normal man could do this, the varying degrees of method and belief in their practices are numerous.

If you've been having a run of bad luck with your health, they might've recommended a certain herb or concoction for the illness but also may have advised taking castor oil for a number of days, due to the belief that castor oil helps purge the body of impurities, including jinxes and tricks. Certain tricks were also hidden in food and found their way into the body by polluting the blood or stomach. In Appalachian folk medicine, many still believe that diseases can be caused by many things: dead animals, tainted food, bathroom fumes, ancestors, demons, spells. The blood allegedly becomes polluted by organic matter that comes into the body via the air or food and drink. This can set up imbalances in the body or cause food to get lodged in the intestines and begin to rot, setting the stage for disease. Here also dietary restrictions may be given. For example, some say don't eat chocolate or drink coffee because it can make rheumatism or arthritis worsen.

Back in the day, tricks such as powdered spider eggs, horsehair, and other such things were introduced into someone's food to conjure them. Spider eggs were often cooked into dumplings or powdered in with ice cream, so again dietary restrictions were advised if this was thought to be the suspect. The work then gets in the body and pollutes it, and the person becomes "rooted," "witched," or "hexed."

Conjure and folk magic sometimes crossed into the realm of the yarb doctor or herb healer, and they also used herbs, purgatives, and washes to help expel "roots" from the body. The yarb or root doctor could be seen praying or reciting Bible verses while creating teas, salves, or compresses, or doing divination, to understand the severity of the person's illness and to see if they'd make it. (The most common form of divination throughout the hills was tea or coffee readings. These were often done for entertainment during hog killings, wakes, and house bees, a time when the whole neighborhood came together to help build a home for a family from hewn logs.)

The cow or horse doctor sometimes employed not only herbs but also prayers, and sometimes knew a thing or two about curing the evil eye or witchcraft when a cow gave bloody milk or a horse couldn't stand. In this way, some would take an herb, usually powdered with other things, and either put it in a wound, give it in drinking water, or dust the animal from head to tail to cure the ailment, whether of physical or spiritual origin.

The witchdoctor primarily cured the effects of witchcraft or conjure in both people and animals; however, he was oftentimes also a root worker or conjurer who folks would go to for luck in money, love, and court cases, among other things, including curses. The practices of the conjurer in the South varied greatly, especially coming into the early twentieth century, when products such as powders and oils were marketed to the public in drugstores and specialty shops alike. Along with these, one could find guidebooks telling you how to win the lottery with lucky numbers in dream books; curio catalogues professing the powers of roots and charms such as a lucky rabbit's foot or galax root; and other books showing you how to work spells or black magic with lamps and candles. Among these titles were *Pow-Wows or Long Lost Friend* by John George Hohman, *The Guide to Health* by Ossman & Steel, *Egyptian Secrets* by Albertus Magnus, *The Sixth and Seventh Books of Moses* (highly taboo), and *Ten Lost Books of the Prophets*. My grandfather had a couple volumes of this last one, which contained the magical knowledge of Solomon, Jesus, and others. He also owned a book called *The Guiding Light to Power and Success* by Mikhail Strabo, which spoke of using candles and Bible verse to achieve love, success, and money, and to curse one's enemies. These books were highly marketed, and contained influences from many cultures. This may help explain why the guidance and methods contained within them continued to be used in some communities decades after they were originally published. I wouldn't put it past folks to have taken up a couple of these and simply started conjuring, along the way professing their power over the competition, especially in the urban areas such as Knoxville.

Next on our list: the witch finder. The witch finder specialized in not only doctoring the witchcraft afflicting a person but also in finding the person who sent it. Whether it was using a picture of the suspect nailed to a tree, a wire hoop, or cutting with a knife the urine or milk of the afflicted, the witch finder's specialty was drawing the witch to come forth no matter what in order to visit the home, usually to borrow an item such as salt, sugar, or bread—anything to keep a charm over the afflicted person. Once a work has been undone or reversed, the ties that were used (such as hair, nail clippings, or worn clothes) become useless. The witchdoctor has called their spirit back from the item and it's no longer tied to the person, which warrants another visit to the person's home to try to get something else to "keep a hold on them." For this reason it was often said to keep from lending any item from the home or allowing the same to be stolen for some time, usually nine days—otherwise the witch finder's charm would be rendered useless as the witch regained power over the victim.

Those born with the sight are said to be able to speak with the dead and have knowledge of events in the past, present, or future. Many conjuring folk with the sight will do little more with their Gift than warn family and friends or possibly read for people. These are the fortune-tellers and prophets. They may knowingly take up this work, or it's possible they won't know of it and will often end up being a top person in the church who speaks prophecies over people or their situations, bringing the Holy Spirit through to enact change. In this way, they would use a form of conjuring by bringing in not just any spirit but The Spirit for a person. By speaking prophecies or testifying, they use the spoken words as their prayers and petitions and enactments on the situation. Not only saying what will be, but ensuring it as well.

The conjurer, root worker, or hex doctor, according to folk belief and stories, was the most feared figure in the community, next to the witch. He was tolerated because folks were under the assumption that he didn't get his powers from the Devil, but they were still cautious around him and sometimes when speaking of him. Conjure folk weren't always equated with the Devil, but they weren't exactly seen sitting in the pews on Sunday, either. This scared folks more because they didn't know for certain who the conjurer "answered to," who his "master" was. In truth, he had no master; he worked for himself. He worked roots and minerals and animal parts into sachets and powders to employ the root, either for or against you, all the while whispering and muttering charms, enchantments, and statements known only to him and the spirits he kept company with. The conjurer knew the spirits much like you know your family members, because often they *were* his family—ghosts of ancestors long gone and recently left, who aided, advised, and consoled him. With these roots and the know-how of twisting nature's hand, he could bring money or love, favor in court, or illness to your enemies (or you).

Even the law had trouble getting these folks for practicing medicine without a license, as in the case of the famous Dr. Buzzard. The conjure man was the hillside Capone for folks here. Don't mess with him, and he won't mess with you. And if anyone came looking for such a person with bad intentions, folks kept their lips zipped because they believed that what the doctor had done for them could be undone just as quickly.

A COMMUNITY STANDARD

Some only worked "good" magic, while others worked tongue-in-cheek on those who did them wrong. It was a popular belief in all of the South that God has just as much to do with fortune as you do, so if something bad happened to your enemies, it was in His will. The conjurer is the person folks turn to when they believe they have been cursed. Family and friends think they have gone crazy and the medical doctors can't figure out why their legs are swelling or their guts feel like they're being pulled out. The conjure doctor was the last resort for many—and still is. Runs of bad luck and illness can decimate a person's entire livelihood here, and for Appalachian Americans, God's timing just isn't quick enough sometimes—so they'd go to the conjure man or woman's house to see what was the matter and to persuade the spirits.

Now people of this profession often exemplified many of these attributes of conjurer, witchdoctor, and witch finder. Some conjurers or root workers simply used herbs in a spiritual way, showing no regular use of their medicinal value aside from the common household remedies folks are raised on in our culture. Some conjurers can not only cure witchcraft or find out who did it, they can also "put the witch under" (in the grave) using their same work. Other times, folks were simply witchdoctors, like Ed McTeer of South Carolina, who only used "white witchcraft," as he called it, to remove the curses and jinxes of other doctors in the area. A reversal isn't guaranteed, though; some people could find out a witch or person behind the matter but didn't have the capability of reversing the work.

Witches were viewed with disdain in much of southern Appalachia. In every community, there was always one person, male or female, who was not trusted or accepted by the rest of the community for one reason or another, which is often inflated as stories get passed down. The community believed this outcast person shouldn't be trusted because they were odd and kept to themselves, which usually lead to the accusation that they were dealing with the Devil for their powers of spells and knowing. Sometimes this was normal bias, while other times it was racially fueled, as is the case of many melungeon families accused back then as can be seen in the stories collected by Hubert Davis in *The Silver Bullet*. Here's the kicker: Appalachian witches were conjurers and root workers as we can see from the old stories of them entertaining spirits and of folks going to them to get roots for money and love as well as cursing—the same work of the accepted conjurer or root worker. That's not to say everybody just loved the conjurer up and down; they were simply held at a better status in the community than the witch. Folks tolerated them and the idea of what they did. However, caution was thick in the air of the communities when it came to conjurers and witchdoctors because some of them were said to "turn" from God and "have the Devil whisper in their ear," or work with both, although their titles rarely changed after the fact. But what about the witch? Only the most desperate would go to them. Most folks would've rather had a conjurer come stay in their home, cooked them food, and had them eat at their table than have anything to do with a witch.

THE FOLK WITCH

So both the conjurer and the witch did the same works. They used the same roots and worked for the same causes. They visited the same graveyards and crossroads and oftentimes dealt with the same spirits. The only distinction ever seen in the old folk tales and stories, when compared, is the group belief or attitude of the community about that individual and the tales that sprung up around them. We can see the same phenomena occur throughout history across the world where folks held in high regard in the community do the same thing as those at the bottom of the social ladder. The former often gets by without folks batting an eye, while the latter is shunned, called names, excommunicated, and sometimes denied service from shops in town. They are isolated for doing the same acts committed by a "better" man. Sometimes, these allegations were utterly false and the said "witch" wasn't one at all.

Even in the words used we can see this divide: conjure and folk magic, that done by normal folks and those respected in the community never really had a name; faith healers *tried* for someone's health, the practice of the yarb doctor was simply called superstition by their Western medical superiors, and the witchdoctor simply did *work* or *roots* on your behalf. However, when something bad was done to someone spiritually, it was and is called witchcraft, because that name carries the same feeling surrounding the folk witch. It is still witchcraft even if the sender is another respected witchdoctor. While people often mistake the witch for the conjure doctor and vice versa, the witch mostly did works of retaliation in return for wrongs done against her. The conjurer was for hire, furnishing folks with spells to get money, find lost items or livestock, take off witchcraft, or curse folks.

Due to the Civil War, many records were lost or destroyed. It's been proposed that this is why there are only a small handful of witchcraft convictions recorded in southern Appalachia. And there are no written documents detailing the execution of a person as a witch. So in Appalachia it seems the limit of witch hysteria seemed to stay at excommunication and public disgrace for the outcast, with a little religious condemnation on the side.

Furthermore, the person's reputation oftentimes was never founded on what they actually did, but on the assumptions and exaggerations of the superstitious community. This is where baby-eating, broom-flying witches come from. These exaggerations often included the Appalachian folk witch turning into an animal, such as a solid black or white cat, a white deer, a boar, a turkey, or a possum, just to name a few. This also included impossible acts such as flying through keyholes and witches slipping from their skin to ride people at night, which was the explanation for people sleepwalking. Other tales detail how one can become a witch, such as by shooting a homemade silver bullet at the full moon while renouncing the Almighty, or standing on the oldest grave and renouncing the Church in order to meet the Devil.

We cannot truly know the practices and methods employed by the folk witch because nobody would associate with them. All we have to go on are exaggerated tales created for entertainment, and a few firsthand accounts. We could compare their stories to similar accounts of yarb and conjure doctors, though, which often have more footing in the real world and outnumber those of the folk witch. They did, after all, do the same works.

Aside from the convicting and often impossible activities of the witch, elements of folk magic were and are largely used by the common people, such as hanging a horseshoe above the door for luck and to avert witches, or keeping a jar of money by the door to draw prosperity. However, some things require professional aid from someone trained in the higher manners of conjure. That's when folks turn to the root worker or witchdoctor, someone more powerful than they are in creating change and moving roots. They're the ones born for it because they have the Gift. Just like jobs, we have specialties about us. Some folks are better at working roots for justice or money, as opposed to protection or love for other people. I myself am better at protection than I am at love work. But back in the day folks often made their living off this, so they were a bit territorial over their area and their clientele and wouldn't often recommend another worker.

STORIES AS TEMPLATES AND GUIDES

Tales of witchcraft and conjuring in Appalachia are a lot of times exaggerated for the storytelling, and over time the truth can become twisted or changed. However, we can find the meaning behind certain things by comparing them to similar tales. This is what I like to call root culture: a set of similar scenes, problems, solutions, and practices seen in the witch and conjure stories of the South. This not only applies to tales from Appalachia but also the Carolina coasts, the Gulf Coast, the Ozarks, and the southern Plains. Folk stories take on lives of their own, and they've got cousins and sisters and twins in every part of the world. By examining their underlying themes, we can better come to a parent belief of the times.

First, we need to establish that the majority of the tricks and formulas used in Appalachia—at least some component of them—are sympathetic in nature, such as gathering dirt from a working railroad, especially as the train passes (which isn't safe or recommended), to send someone or something away. We also see in many tales that witches can be killed or brought out of hiding through sympathetic means. These are sometimes the same methods employed by the conjurers as well.

Methods for Killing or Harming a Witch

A widely dispersed method of killing a witch was to draw a picture of the witch on a piece of paper, wood, or cardboard, nail the image to a tree, and shoot it with a silver bullet, usually fashioned from old dimes or quarters, which had a high silver content back then. Wherever the drawing received damage, the witch would as well, so their injuries outed them as a witch to the victim.

One story from my family's old homestead in Tipton Hill, North Carolina, was of a woman by the name of Pheobe Lingerfeltz of Pigeon Roost. The story, as related by my Mamaw Hopson's neighbor, Harvey Miller, is a first-person account of him hunting for turkeys in the woods. Each time, there was one turkey in particular that would sneak up on him and mess up his aim when trying to shoot one of the birds. So he fired at this persistent turkey, close enough that missing was logically impossible. But each time he missed. He figured the turkey must be a witch turkey, so he took it upon himself to craft a silver bullet, the only thing said to be able to kill a witch, and set out again. When he saw the turkey, he again took aim and fired away, harming the turkey in the leg. It got away before he could finish the job. A few days later, word came to him of a woman up the holler who had "took to the bed" due to severe rheumatism in her leg. The woman was Pheobe, the turkey witch, and she walked with a limp for the rest of her life.

Another story, coming from Wise County, Virginia, recounts a time when a farmer's cow gave bloody milk after a woman had come by and said how "mighty fine" the animal was. A friend recommended cutting a square piece of pig meat from the left hind leg and heating it on the stove on low. By the time the meat begins to cook, the witch would be knocking at the door. Well, sure enough, there was a knock at the door about an hour after the meat was put on. A woman asked if she could borrow the plow. The farmer told her his neighbor had it, and she left. But in a bit there was another knock at the door. This time the woman was obviously fidgeting and impatient. "You got any fresh water?" she asked. The farmer told her the bucket hadn't been brought from the well yet, so she took her leave. That piece of meat continued getting hotter and hotter until it started baking, at which point the farmer saw the woman running down the road heading toward the house, holding her shoulder. She barged in the door and pointed at the stove. "Take that damn thing out of there or you're gonna kill me!"

She revealed her shoulder, and sure enough it was as crisp and cooked as the meat in the oven.

Head and Foot Rites

We can also take into account head and foot rites, where the space between the crown of the head and the soles of the feet are the measurements of the person and are specific to them. The head and feet are also a spiritual entry point, for blessings or curses. We see this applied in one witch tale, which has different variations based on location. The tale says that to become a witch you have to go up to the highest hill in the area at dawn and say Bible verses backward as the sun rises. Either the Devil or one of his witches will appear and place one hand on your head and one on the bottom of your left foot. They will then ask you to renounce the Lord and dedicate all that lays between their hands to the Devil and his works.

So here the placement of the hands on the head and feet are being used in an agreement or contract, with the measurement of the person being not only the collateral but also the physical contract. This leads to the popular belief in witch marks—places on the body that indicate one is a witch and in league with Satan. Witch marks could be black moles, odd growths, or other strange markings or scars on the body. For melungeon people accused of such, the sign was usually being born polydactyl. In the above story, a witch mark would be the "signature" on the contract. These stories are largely exaggerated, but if there's a bit of truth in them, then these elements of the tales, such as a high place, hands on the head and feet, and the time of sunrise can be tied to other stories and further connected to old-time remedies and charms that have been recorded by folks who didn't profess themselves as witches.

Other Indicators of a Witch

The idea of markings on the body indicating witchcraft or devilment never really took hold in Appalachia. Rather, it was how someone dressed or acted, including strange combinations of their genetics, such as hair, skin, and eye color. In Appalachia, this could include an African American with red hair and blue eyes, or a person with eyes that changed color later in life, another reasoning applied to melungeon witches.

Still, certain attitudes and behaviors could apparently give away a witch's acts, such as refusing any neighbor or person who asked to borrow anything, regardless of the article in need. This was sometimes done by a lot of folks, but usually only concerning salt, butter, milk, or flour—things that nourish the home and family—and usually this was only done when someone in the home had been "shot" or afflicted with witchcraft and they were at that time waiting for the witch to come as the witch finder forced them out to come to the home. No, the one named a witch for this behavior always did this, regardless of the item needed or current events in the community. Folks say this was so she could "keep her power."

It was said in Tennessee that the simple presence of a witch made the milk sour overnight. A lot of folks in Washington, Carter, Greene, Unicoi, and Scott counties used to hold the belief that people who gazed and stared off at nothing a lot or wore a red handkerchief were witches. This is sometimes found in other witch stories as well, and I have seen Nana Trivett stare off often before saying something that would in time come true or be validated. It is a practice I call gazing.

Witches were also said to make strange noises—ones that could be heard from their house or their land, ones that didn't mimic any other animal and often sent chills up the spine. Again, this may simply be an exaggeration, or it could have been explained by a cougar being in heat, long before they were deemed "extinct" here. The sound of that animal can be chilling to the bone, and considering cougars and big cats were one of the witch's forms, it's reasonable that its scream would be associated with death and witchcraft.

So this is the array of spiritual practitioners that have been hidden away behind gravestones and church pews. Some of this is taboo and some of it is accepted in the culture. The lines between the two are just a bit thicker than that between the conjurer and the witch. Other books have been written on faith healing and historical herbal medicine practices in Appalachia, but the spiritual natures of the roots and things have often been overlooked or deemed taboo. We are forgetting the doctors who helped and cured us when there was no one else! Nowadays, folks think it's all superstition. But behind closed doors, folk still believe there's something always in the dark, watching and waiting. They still believe in curses and demons and that there are ways to get rid of them. But lord, how do you do it? They don't know, because it's slipping away from the culture.

So, what of the conjurers and the inner workings of their roots and tricks? Guard your spirit and keep your shoes on! The roots we may find could be familiar or altogether foreign, depending on where in the South you're from, and not all of them may be benign.

2

CATCHING SPIRITS

Now that we've seen what kind of folks did this work, by what degrees, and with what kind of spiritual assistance, we need to understand the beliefs behind the work: the way the order of things works in our eyes. Appalachian folk magic and conjure were born from a mindset that's fearful of the unknown, a trait passed down from the ancestors of Europe, Africa, and the New World. Residing here is also the imagination, that mechanism that has guided man in some of his greatest feats. Then we also have faith and religion, which give direction and boundaries to the fear and imagination; they act as barriers and law makers. Stories take on a primary role here as well. Stories define us and give us guidance.

Storytelling has been a huge part of our culture for centuries and has played a major role in the area for millennia with the Yuchi, the Cherokee, African Americans, and European immigrants. Storytelling is a worldwide phenomenon. It has guided us from the beginning of our species and it still does, as long as we listen. Storytelling is the meeting point of faith and reality. It explains and defines and records experiences and histories, the realness of which is never debated. True or not, they are always true. If even one person can relate to a story, it is true and will remain so.

Our ancestors feared what was in the night: ghosts that screamed and bled, black beasts with red eyes that prowled the woods, and witches that watched from the keyhole as you slept, waiting to saddle you up and ride to town. The mind of the mountaineer was filled with tales of glory and miracles, but also of terror and witchcraft. Whether it's stories of a plant's powerful medicine or tales of a phantom dog disappearing into a cloud of rags, anything is possible in these hills.

The greatest threat to our livelihood was and still sometimes is sickness and death. As noted before, these could be caused by diseases that originated in a normal manner, but the most dreaded were those that did not have a natural origin. Those sharp pains in the feet and sides, the vomit or urine, and the untimely death of a loved one could be the result of witchcraft! Remember that anything sent against you for a malice cause is witchcraft, regardless of the nature or title of the one who sent it. It's like chemicals: used in a medical lab, it is medicine; but used to kill many people, it is biochemical warfare.

Human beings are vulnerable creatures. We can achieve great things to the point that we forget our fragility. That fragility was far worse a hundred years ago than it is now. Just about every culture and people throughout history have seen and understood this; they taught that balance for the human body, mind, and soul is vital to health. Just the littlest thing can set you off balance and make you ill or susceptible to unseen dangers. The Cherokee understood this, the immigrants did as well, and the modern mountaineer still knows it. In the study of folk magic, it is apparent that there are layers to it based on public knowledge and usage. Folk magic formulas become superstitions and taboo when spread and used widely by the layfolk. They aren't regarded as charms but more simply as omens or tales that begin with, "It's good luck to . . ." "It's bad luck for . . ." or "If such and such happens . . ." They are widely dispersed and in most part are the sole reason many of these teachings have remained, albeit with many variations.

The belief in witchcraft and sickness or trouble from haints (troublesome spirits) was a widespread superstition and still is. For this reason, in just about every collection of American folklore you look at you will find references to keeping haints and witches out or how to detect and defeat them. They were and still can be a primary danger to one's way of life. Here resides the horseshoe above the door and salt lines at the doors and windows. As time has marched on, people have fallen out of these practices. They have forgotten the stories and are more vulnerable to the things that sent chills up their great-granny's spine at night. We have become blind.

But we did see once upon a time the inner mechanism of the natural world that covers and surrounds these mountains. Everything has a tale to tell, such as why women rule the house, why the possum's tail is hairless, why the blue jay's legs are burnt, where the balds on the mountains came from. Everything is connected and has played out a story up to today; and the story is still going, but no one's watching anymore.

BALANCE AND CONDITIONS

Because everything is connected, anything can affect and change another thing. This is the basis for most of Appalachian folk magic and conjure. Like affects like, or like actions create like causes. Our folk medicine and faith follow these lines as well: for example, what can kill you can cure you—or, as the old folks say, the hair of the dog that bit you. This is an actual cure for a dog bite: take the hair from the tip of its tail and rub it in the wound. This has evolved in the present day to drinking a shot of alcohol to cure a hangover.

Cold, heat, moisture, and dryness also play a role in folk magic, medicine, and conjure. These can create imbalances in the body. Coldness increases phlegm, while heat increases blood. Moisture increases yellow bile, while dryness increases black bile. You are susceptible to cold or the flu if you go outside in the winter with a wet head: coldness from the air and heat from your body increases phlegm in the lungs as well as blood production, which can increase the likelihood of you getting sick. The risk is further exacerbated by a quick or extreme change in temperature. Mama explained that the reason you're not supposed to swim soon after eating is that hot meals that give off steam (moisture) increase both yellow and black bile, which also increases blood and can cause bloated ears and cramping while swimming. Simply too much is going on with the body between digestion and exertion in the pool.

Following these theories of the balances of the body, folk magic and conjure that are aimed at it can be timed and used the same way, along with following the signs, because the spirit is just as vulnerable as the body. For example, if you wanted to place a root on a person by them stepping over it and have it act quickly, you would make up the powder when the moon is in the sign of the feet (Pisces), wetting it with water and then allowing it to dry (following the sticky nature of phlegm, things attach to it). Wait for a hot, humid day, when the blood is rushing and phlegm is up from the moisture, to lay the powder. The day should also still be in the time when the sign is in the feet, as whatever sign governs the day, that part of the body is most vulnerable and the blood can settle there (which, according to the old theories, can create sickness due to settled or bad blood). So here you have a powder made and planted in the sign of the feet on a day when the blood and phlegm, both collectors of foreign matter, are high and when the entry point of the trick is most vulnerable.

CATCHING A SPIRIT

The human spirit can be caught in a trick or root such as a powder or doll baby in many ways. The spirit can be caught by acquiring some water the person has washed in. It can also be taken through pictures of the person, as long as the person in the photo's eyes are open, better if looking right at the camera.

The feet are also a vulnerable point for the spirit, because they are the foundation of the body and are where we're "tied up," since the feet come out last when we're born. For this reason, foot tracks are taken up for various purposes, such as performing love work, bringing bad luck, cursing, healing, and more. To do ill, the track in the dirt was picked up usually from heel to toe or just from the heel—the Achilles' heel of their spirit, so to speak. For benign works, it is taken up from toe to heel. Certain parts of the track represent specific aspects of the person's life: their love life is in the last three little toes; their health is in their heel; their money and luck are in the first two toes. Working by this, if you wanted to help bring money to someone, you would take up their track on just the inner side, where the two first toes would be, from toe to heel. (Remember, toe to heel to bring or attract, and heel to toe to send out or away.) Back in the old days, roads were mostly gravel and dirt, so it was no issue to take up the dirt from someone's tracks. But today everything is covered in concrete. To adapt to this, my family uses a damp washcloth or hankie and wipes in the same fashion as we would picking up actual dirt, based on direction and area concerning the intentions of the work.

Your spirit can also be caught up or captured in hair, nails, urine, and blood—really, anything that comes from your body or that has been in contact with it in an "intimate" fashion. This might include soiled or dirty clothes, napkins used for wiping scabs or to clean the nose, rags with intimate fluids on them, such as semen or vaginal fluid, and shoes. This is based on the belief that like affects like, except here the fetish is you or a part of you in some form. These things contain your essence and bits of your spirit. They are even more tightly tied to you than your name, although names are also used—so is your birthday and time of birth. All these things come together to identify one individual; you are the only you, and that makes you vulnerable.

Next on the list is your property: the place you eat, sleep, and live. It's filled with you. This is the basis behind what we saw earlier in getting something that belonged to the person through borrowing, leaving ownership to the person you want to work on. Because of southern hospitality, when you borrow something, folks usually say, "I'll pay you back" or something of that nature, to which the usual response is, "Don't worry about it," which is them giving it to you. "Thank you" and "You're welcome" should be all that is said. This is probably the main reason this phenomenon didn't carry over to Appalachia well: we are caring people who like to help anyone out. You hear more tales of hair and nail clippings, of dolls and blood, than you do of using borrowed items. The closest thing that could be related is the requirement of an item to be stolen as a loophole around this, should all other possibilities fail. Generally, these aren't used, as they aren't as strong as hair, blood, bodily fluids, or names.

Things could be laid in your tracks or places you'll pass or even on your property, whether hidden in the house or buried in the ground, to have power over you. Dirt from your property could also be used, and is why folks would move furniture around a couple times a year. This changes the essence of the home and can help guard against witchcraft done with dirt from your yard.

Other things used to be done to cover up the trails left of your spirit to guard against capturing. Most folks used to burn their hair and nails, lest they fall into the wrong hands. They'd also burn bandages that contained their blood, or make sure that they were disposed of in a way that no one could get a hold of them. You'd also never leave your dirty laundry sitting out, lest someone come and steal something without you knowing it. It's also common to wash the bottoms of your shoes upon returning home. Many folks were told this kept the house clean, which it did, but that's the thing with this work: everything is done for two or three reasons. If your hair gets used in a bird's nest, you'll have a headache as long as the bird sits there; if ants find your nails and take them to their nest, you'll be hard on money; and washing your shoes cleans them and keeps the house clean. My family has always cut our own hair and the women always did their own nails. To this day I've never been to a barber; either I cut my own hair or my mother cuts it for me.

My mother also washed the doors and windows and walls with ammonia, vinegar, and lemon in water to not only cleanse and strip away bad or settled stuff, but also physically clean the walls and windows. We also burned Indian House Blessing incense, usually found in dollar stores, to not only make the house smell good but also bring money or peace. Nana never used incense because of her allergies, but her mother-in-law, Mamaw Seagle, burned a certain mixture on her stove every so often that gave off a sweet, musk smell; I recon for the same double reasons.

TIMING AND WEATHER

The earth and the weather have an effect on conjuring and this is paid attention to when working roots or working with spirits. This is old conjure information that many folks today don't know of and don't share, but it needs to be shared with the resurrection of Appalachian folk magic and conjure. Contacting spirits is best done at night, especially when the humidity or moisture levels are up. Spiritually, heat, cold, moisture, and dryness work about the same here, but only on "essence," as Nana said. (We used the word *essence* for the makeup of spirits.) This is the reason many spiritual encounters, often those scary stories you hear about, happen at nighttime, when there's an increase in essence and it isn't being cut down by the sun's energy. Moisture and coolness generally increase essence while heat and dryness decrease it, although there are some accounts where the presence of a ghost or haint is detected by a warm spot. The large majority of spirit and phantom appearances occur at night, usually when there are clouds, when steam is rising off the roads beneath the street lights, or when there's a fog rolling in.

We also work with the phases of the moon when dealing with the dead. If you wish to contact a deceased relative who has been dead for . . .

- Less than a year, do work between the new moon and the first quarter;
- One to three years, do work between the waxing crescent and the first quarter;
- Three to seven years, do work between the first quarter and the waxing gibbous;
- Seven to ten years, do work between the waxing gibbous and the second day of the full moon;
- Ten to fifteen years, do work between the last day of the full moon and the waning gibbous;
- Fifteen to twenty-five years, do work between the waning gibbous and the last quarter;
- Twenty-five to forty years, do work between the last quarter and the waning crescent;
- More than forty years, do work between the waning crescent and the new moon.

My family tradition follows this by the basis that graveyard dirt has a sinking quality, and over time it anchors anything buried in it. This is mapped with the rise and fall of the moon phases, going upward to the surface of the ground and downward again. Aside from moon phases, timing and dates can also be beneficial in making contact. Contacting the deceased on their birthday, wedding anniversary, or anniversary of their death are best, with the latter being the strongest because it was the last "door" in life used by the spirit. The times of 10 P.M., 11 P.M., 12 A.M., and 3 A.M. are also popular in spirit lore, "between times" when neither sun nor moon are at their highest or between days, in the case of midnight.

With root working and conjure, roots and tricks are best laid or done at certain times. Roots that will enter through the feet are best laid when the earth is wet; this is also the best time to take up foot tracks. Your foot track shows where you've been, where you are, and where you're going. Because of this, foot track work has to be done quickly, before the next rains, or all the foot tracks made since last rainfall will be washed away and the root will have a hard time finding the person.

Candles

Candles are best worked and burned in hot, dry weather because there's little moisture or water for the candle to "beat up against" on its way off. Just make sure it's warm and there's at least one cloud in the sky—no clouds means "both heaven and earth are dry and closed up," according to Nana. Humidity levels can affect the candle's burn as well. If the work isn't urgent, have a bit of patience and wait for a good hot and dry day to start. The days following may be a battle, depending on the weather, but the pathway was well set, so it's more likely to work. For workings that are urgent, go by the rise and fall of the sun or by the hands of the clock: to bring or attract, work when the sun or hand is going up; to send away, avert, or bring down, work when the hand is going down.

Powders

Powders are best made when there are clouds in the sky and the earth is cool to the touch. I also pay attention to insect activity, because they can mess up powders by walking through them once they've been laid. I'll sit and watch a patch of earth for about ten minutes. If I don't see many insects and the conditions are right, I'll get to work. This is something spirit showed me personally and is not necessarily traditional.

Washes and Oils

Washes and oils are best made and used right after it rains due to the moisture in the air. They are less likely to wear off too quickly in heat or warm weather if the humidity is high, and the air feels sticky.

Poke Bags

The most complicated root is the poke bag or sachet, known in other regions as a toby, hex bag, jack, jack ball, mojo bag, gris-gris, or hand. It is a pouch of fabric, either sewn or tied, usually of flannel or some worn cloth, which contains roots and other curios that are paired together and "baptized" and even "named" for a certain reason, such as protection, drawing love or money, or bringing ruin to your enemies. Poke bags are the most delicate of roots and charms in Appalachian folk magic due to the rules and taboos of caring for them. Poke bags need to be fed in order to continue working; this keeps the essence or energy going for the work. They are usually fed by dusting them with baby powder or flour, or rubbing them with chewing dip or snuff. They can also be fed with bodily fluids such as urine or sweat, or drinks such as whiskey or moonshine.

Poke bags must never be touched by anyone but their owner, and some go as far as saying they should never be seen by anyone else. My family has seen my bags and they work fine. The only issue I've found is when a stranger sees them. Regardless, no one else is allowed to touch one of my poke bags. Doing so would "kill" it in the sense that the fetish spirit called into it during its making will no longer return to the bag. Its home has been invaded and desecrated, so it will need to be called back to a new home, a new bag or the same one that has been washed and reconstructed. Some folks also think that if a poke or hex bag touches the ground, then that will kill it as well; however, in my experience a couple soft drops don't hurt much, but a hard one will. Like I said, it's the tiny spirit's home (imagine what your house would look like if dropped softly as opposed to harshly).

The longer you keep your bag fed, the stronger it will get. Now, should you forget to feed it, it is not unusual for it to seek a "drink" for itself, so they may turn up missing sometimes. Other times, they may wander off to act out their jobs. The rabbit's foot that I carry once disappeared from my pocket as I slept and was finally found outside at the edge of the property, seemingly guarding the place from someone or something.

REASONS AND BELIEF

So what makes a root tick? How does a sack of horsehair, roots, needles, and thorns have an effect on someone or something? We believe that everything is connected and mirrors aspects of human life. Every plant was given its medicine by the Creator, and the cure for a poisonous plant is always found growing nearby.

Animals also have their own medicine, so to speak: hog teeth and mouse teeth were used to help someone withstand and overcome a toothache because the animals' teeth are very strong and not easily broken.

The same applies to plants, based on a belief called the doctrine of signatures, which states that every plant has a physical characteristic that acts as a key or code to its use by man. So a plant with heart-shaped leaves may be medicine for troubles of the heart or used in love charms; kidney beans may help with kidney trouble or be used to filter bad stuff out, or clear a path of troubles.

The uses of a plant in folk medicine and folk magic are sometimes similar but are mostly drastically different. Dandelion root is taken as a tonic for general health but may also be carried for the same thing, especially for strength. Black cohosh root is used to ease symptoms of menopause in women, while in conjuring it is a great aid in curing conjure-sickness or tricks placed against you. The reasons behind a root's use, or the use of zoological curios, are numerous. It could be a root is part of an old superstition from a long-forgotten story, it played a part in a folk story handed down, or a connection is simply made in the mind of a mountaineer through observation. One prime example of this would be kudzu, an invasive vine that was brought here from overseas. It has no predators here, so it is able to grow freely and rather quickly, up to a foot a day, thus covering everything in its path and choking out any competition, including bushes and towering trees. Because of this, kudzu leaves are used to conquer enemies and prevent conjuring from getting to you, and the root is carried for success and strength.

There's a charm for strong working hands that's mole feet worn around the neck, because the mole is able to dig into the hard earth with ease. An old cure for colic was a tea made from the inner linings of chicken gizzards, the reason being the gizzards are hard and sturdy, using grit to break up food and would make the child strong enough to overcome the colic and crud by sympathetically breaking up the crud. It was also believed that eating cooked minnows helped cure alcoholism: the person will no longer drink like a fish, just like the fish won't once it's cooked.

Household items are also used in folk magic and medicine: knives or scissors for cutting or severing, nails for harming or securing something in place, and cleaning products such as vinegar, ammonia, or laundry bluing to clean both physically and spiritually. Even soda pop was used. Called "dope" back in the old days in smaller communities, it could be used to "sweeten" a person to you or, if left long enough, "eat them up" with worry and stress should it be used on an enemy. Light sodas were generally used for the former, while darker sodas were used for the latter.

FREEING THE SPIRIT

The ways in which the human spirit can be trapped or released by conjure are numerous. By the old saying, fight fire with fire, this is done to free the spirit. Just as the spirit has been caught by sympathetic means, it can also be released by sympathetic means. For example, say someone buried a root for you to walk over and ever since then you have been racked with pains, sleeplessness, moodiness, glazed eyes, or nightmares. The usual prescription back in the day would be to hire a witchdoctor to find the root, douse it in moonshine and vinegar or salt, and either burn it or throw it in running water, such as a creek or stream. Nowadays, yards are smaller, so if you don't find the root there, lord knows where it could be planted. With everybody going every which way—that way, this way, over there, over here—it would be hell to try to retrace all your steps in the past month. My family gets around this by burning the shoes and burying the ashes at a crossroads or throwing them in running water before cleansing or bathing.

Once trapped, the human spirit is broken or under confinement, inside the root put against you if it's a poke bag, doll, or jar. With powders, smoke, and oils (contagious roots), the trick is planted on you and is just along for the ride with its claws dug into your back. Freeing the spirit from the latter is quite easy with a few baths and washings, perhaps a change of clothes, and a haircut. The harder part is freeing the spirit from a bottle, doll, or bag. When the spirit is held hostage like this, under a curse or other working against the mind, behaviors change and so does the balance of the body. Illnesses develop that are only worsened by Western medicine. In many tales, the more medicine a person takes, the closer they come to dying unless a witchdoctor or conjurer is able to come cure them and restore their spirit.

There are several ways to determine if a root has been planted against you, what kind of root it is, and how to destroy it. Following are a few ways in which the spirit can be released. Generally, bottles and jars are broken and any personal concerns such as hair or nails are burned. Poke bags are burned, dismantled by opening and removing all the objects, or are thrown into a creek or river. It is common to see the latter done when not only is the spell reversed but the conjurer or witch is sent away, out of town, far away from the victim.

Candles that have been used against you can be "put out" in a number of ways:

- Write your name on a piece of paper and put it in a plastic bag filled with your bathwater. Hang the bag from a branch above an upturned pot, on the bottom of which you have written the name of the witch or simply "All my enemy's works." Prick the bag with a new sewing needle in a gentle manner to let a small bit of water drip out and into the pot. Let this continue until the bag is empty.

- Get a plain white taper candle and on it write the witch's name or "All my enemy's works," carving from top to bottom. Cut the tip of the candle off, snip the wick flush with the wax, and flatten the bottom so the candle has two bottoms now. Turn to the original bottom and cut through it about 1 centimeter from the end, avoiding the wick. You should now have a new top. Set this in a candle holder. Burn the candle as the sun goes down, and bury the remains at a crossroads far from your house. Return without looking back. (Note: When destroying bad roots, never look back. Folks report hearing the mimicked voices of family members calling them back, or the screams and wailing of some creature, or even laughter. *Don't look back.*)

If your spirit has been trapped in a doll baby, you'll need to dis-associate from it as much as possible: cut your hair, color it, or change the style; change your shoes; keep your nails short; change your perfume or cologne; and change your eating habits. Do this for at least a month, and eventually the root will tire itself out trying to find you, trying to connect. Roots and tricks run on the account of predictability and patterns. They see you coming and they know where you're going.

You can also try going to church on Sunday with a quarter. Stand at the altar, place the quarter beneath your left shoe, and pray: "I am the only one, I am the only I that I am. I am the one knitted in my mother's womb by three hands: the Father, the Son, and the Holy Spirit," or something along those lines decreeing you are the only one of you that should be.

This all seems a bit cut and dry in our modern times, fanciful even. But these things posed a dire threat to the livelihood of many people and simultaneously were the bedrock of one's luck and success in just acquiring enough food for a month. These stories also show the conjurer at work as well as the faith healer and witchdoctor. Let's meet them.

3

RED ROOTS

In this chapter, we will see many fantastic things and meet people of this region. There were too many recorded tales of Appalachian workers to include here, so I chose those stories that demonstrate methods and practices of a similar manner as those employed and generally seen in the Appalachian regions both north and south. We will also see how the lines often cross between conjurer, yarb doctor, and faith healer in the tales that follow.

THE RED FOX OF THE MOUNTAINS

I think the most fitting one we should meet first is the well-known Marshall Benton Taylor of Wise County, Virginia: the dreaded "Red Fox" of the mountains. Before we get to his story, I want you to keep in mind that back in his day, law enforcement wasn't as strong as it is today; it didn't have the same reach or capability of physically and readily bringing someone to justice, so some folks took it upon themselves to search out wrongdoers and administer justice outside the formal system.

Marshall "Red Fox" Taylor was born in Scott County on May 8, 1836. Folks all around these parts were terrified of him because he was slicker than a fox and had many a man captured and brought to justice. He was a revenue agent, United States marshal, herb doctor, spiritualist, preacher, and faith healer. He has been described as having a kind, compassionate look on one side of his face and a snarl on the other side, with a twinkle in his eye that told you he was already ahead of you. Folks said that while tracking outlaws, he would hide in the woods on the mountain trails. He'd also cut off the soles of his shoes and reverse them so it appeared that wherever he went, his footprints showed him going the other way.

Some fellows would brag about seeing him and scaring him, trying to tear his name down. One man did so and was walking home one night when he saw out of the corner of his eye the Red Fox was walking beside him. He hadn't heard Red Fox come up, and he never said a word; just gave him a look as if to say, "Watch it." Outlaws would run like hell if they ever found that Red Fox was on their trail because his success rate was basically 100 percent—either dead or alive, they were brought in.

Red Fox studied medicine with his uncle at a time when there weren't any colleges around, so he was book learned and a faith healer. He often prescribed charms along with herbs to enact a cure and would tell folks to sit and pray while he went outside, where he would stand with arms open to the sky, and if they felt a warm feeling taking over, to call his name. After this, they would be cured of whatever ailed them. It's said he always carried a bag on his saddle filled with herbs that he used to conjure and cure, right alongside his guns. He was also a preacher and spoke often of visions; it's said these aided him in his hunts. He would preach to just about any person or crowd that would have him. But, aside from preaching and curing, he is most famous as an assassin, his legendary name having been born at Killing Rock, where he killed an infamous moonshiner by the name of Ira Mullins due to a personal vendetta between the two.

For this Red Fox was set to be hung—but not before he preached at his own funeral to hundreds in attendance from all over southwestern Virginia. With the Red Fox, his faith was the closest thing to him. In his trial, the judge asked if he had anyone to testify on his behalf. His response was, "Jesus Christ!" He then proceeded to preach, a foreshadowing of sorts that he would also preach at his own hanging, to which he requested to be dressed in solid white. He also claimed that he would rise from the dead three days after burial. In the courtroom, he prayed verses showing his own innocence beneath the Just Judge and also preached damnation to his enemies, who seemingly all died shortly after his own "death." Some rumors persist that he didn't die that day, but rather walked out in the company of some freemason brothers, after which he skipped out to Missouri, while others say he's buried in an unmarked grave in Wise County.

He was a mad man, to say the least, never admitting guilt for the massacre that resulted from his personal vengeance. His body never rose, but folks say the Red Fox of the Mountains is still out there, healing and tricking and praying in spirit.

MAMMY WISE

Mammy Wise (Weiss) saw many things. She resided along the Upper Tennessee–North Carolina border in the late 1800s near Washington and Carter counties in Tennessee, presently known as Unicoi county. She was tall and heavyset, with long, course black hair that looked and felt like hemp rope. She had small, dark eyes and "was dark as an Injun," which may have been on account of melungeon heritage with Indian blood. She cured a multitude of things, including thrush and colic, and her abilities were attributed to the fact that her father died before she was born. While there are some theories that she may have also been a seventh daughter, it is this one fact that seems to be the reason she was able to cure or see: a person who never met their father could cure thrush or colic by blowing in the child's mouth, among other abilities, including the sight. But she not only healed and saw visions, she saw what caused the ailments as well.

She foretold the coming of the Civil War. She said this vision happened when she saw the night sky filled with stars, but a bright star in the north fell and clashed with a bright star in the south, which she interpreted as a war between the North and the South. Just before the war, an omen visited the heavens in 1861 known as a "hairy star" or war comet. Beyond everything she saw and told, this is the fuel of her southern fame to this day.

Aside from this, she also found out thieves. One story goes that a woman's prized jewel necklace had been stolen, so she traveled across the state to meet with Mammy. Mammy got the names of suspects, the usual troublemakers in the community the woman lived in, on a piece of paper and placed it snug at the bottom of a pot of boiling water into which she dropped three dead crawfish. After saying her enchantments over the boiling brew, the breasts of the crawfish opened up and whizzed a name on the list.

In another tale, a family by the name of Johnson took residence along the Davidson River and the man of the home soon sent for Mammy due to the gravel. (He had kidney stones.) When Mammy arrived, it came to her attention that they had hosted a man named Carson who was traveling around. However, Carson returned after finding a large sum of his money missing. Wise divined that Mr. Johnson was the thief and this was the cause of his ailment, an example of "sin" making you sick.

She was also the person folks would go to for "love potions" she would brew up in her kitchen. She'd send them on with a bottle of it and swear they shouldn't let it leave their hands until they got home—otherwise the spirits would fly back home to her.

WITCH MCGAHA

One of the prime examples of a moody, cursing witch in Appalachia is Witch McGaha of the Great Smoky Mountains. What is now Great Smoky Mountain National Park used to be a herd of small communities that no longer exist since the park was set and folks were made to move. Residing near here was Witch McGaha, also known as Squad McGaha, whom neighbors disliked because she was constantly asking to borrow things from everyone, yet she wouldn't let anyone borrow anything from her. Sound familiar? It's said she didn't do without, but for some mysterious reason she needed to borrow things.

One fall, her sister, Nance, asked to get some apples from her orchard but McGaha refused and shooed her away. Nance thought it wise to sneak through and get some apples, but Witch McGaha found her and cursed her, sending Devils in the form of squirrels after her. Nance noticed a pulling at her dress and saw it was a squirrel. Then another tug, and another. Each time she turned around, the number of squirrels had doubled. She began to run, but no matter how fast she ran the squirrels kept scratching and tormenting her until she was a bloody mess. She tried her best to get across the threshold of her doorway at her home, where a broom was laid across to keep out evil, but she died on her porch.

THE POWELL SISTERS

One of my favorite tales growing up was of Irene and Drusilla Powell of Scott County, Virginia, who lived between present-day Hiltons, Virginia, and Bloomingdale, Tennessee, some two hundred years ago. Growing up, they were always getting into trouble—but it wasn't until they were older that things got worse and bloody. Everyone was afraid of them—bootleggers, outlaws, everybody in town. Irene and Drusilla were inseparable; even after they both married and had children, they would go off together to somewhere nobody knew.

Before the bad things began happening everywhere they went, Irene and Drusilla were both trained and effective midwives. Besides their cures and aid, folks also went to them for charms to gain love or luck. After a while of this is when the bad things started happening. See, the Powell Sisters' magic seemed to be a paradox where something was given, but something was taken as well. A woman would gain the affections of her lover, but would become infertile or lose her hair; a man would win every game of chance, but the luckier he got, the worse his health became.

Everywhere the sisters went, folks argued, things fell or broke, and people got sick. Cows caught ill and crops withered. Soon, the few hours they stole away grew longer and longer, until they were gone for days and weeks at a time. It's said they abused their children and tormented their husbands' minds with all kinds of crazy until their folks got fed up and told them to just stay gone for good. So they did.

Isolated in the mountains far away from everyone, the only time the sisters came into town was when they needed something. But now twelve or thirteen stray dogs that they had taken in followed right on their heels. Hunters in town swore the animals were demons in disguise, and that the Powell sisters would sometimes have unnatural relations with them to keep the Devil's bidding up. One day, everything changed when Drusilla went to the well to get water while Irene was out. The dogs turned on her and tore her to shreds. Supposedly this was the "payment" for their powers, an end to their contract of sorts. When Irene came home and found her sister in pieces, she hung herself from a tree.

The folks who found them buried their corpses outside McMurray Cemetery, beyond the bounds of hallowed ground. Since then there have been stories that you can sometimes hear them screaming and beating at the tops of their coffins, with the occasional song of a stressed rope coming from a tree nearby. The dogs never returned.

THE OAK RIDGE PROPHET

Born November 9, 1865, in Oakridge, Tennessee, John Hendrix is known today as a prophet and mystic whose predictions were scarily accurate. He was married to Julia Ann Griffith and they had four children. After their daughter Ethel died of a strange infection in the nose and throat, Julia blamed John for causing the sickness because he had whooped Ethel over something before she got sick. Soon after, John was deserted by his wife and kids, who took off to Arkansas.

Heartbroken, John turned to religion and mysticism. He slept on the ground in the woods for forty days, believing that God would talk to him there. This is when his visions began. He announced his visions and prophecy to his neighbors, but they all deemed him crazy and out of his head. John predicted that his hometown would soon have huge buildings and big engines building something, and it would all be to help stop the biggest war in history. He even gave specific locations of routes and railroads, which have turned out to be true. He spoke of Oak Ridge, the establishment that played a major role in the development of the atomic bomb, and aided the Allies during World War II. John Hendrix wasn't a witch or a conjurer, but a seer: somebody who can see and hear the word of God and spirit. He died of tuberculosis on June 2, 1915.

BOB SHEFFEY

Robert "Bob" Sheffey, born July 4, 1820, was a circuit rider, a traveling preacher who went from town to town sharing the Gospel. Like most circuit riders, he'd stay in some parts for a week or more ministering to the locals. Folks often called him St. Francis of the Wilderness because of the care he showed to animals, even stopping his wagon on mountain trails to relocate a beetle from the wagon's route. He truly detested illicit distilling and would pray curses on folks' stills, asking the Lord to destroy them. For one he prayed against, he asked that a tree fall on it and ruin it. The only problem was that the still wasn't near any trees; but that didn't matter, because a tornado came through and dropped a tree right on it.

But that isn't what Sheffey's most known for. He's known for the curse he made on his hometown in the late 1800s that continues today. When he came riding through Ivanhoe, Virginia, the town was prosperous with a railroad, a rock quarry, and lead mines. In their free time, the locals passed the nights with gambling and drinking and all nature of things that Sheffey found distasteful and bad.

Because of this and the locals' rejection of his ministry and word, upon leaving town Sheffey did as the Bible says in Matthew 10:14–15:

> *14 And whosoever shall not receive you, nor hear your words, when ye depart out of that house or city, shake off the dust of your feet.*
>
> *15 Verily I say unto you, It shall be more tolerable for the land of Sodom and Gomorrah in the day of judgment, than for that city.*

Sheffey took his shoes off and knocked them together while cursing the town, saying Ivanhoe will never amount to anything and will slip into the pits of hell. Since then, all the industries that made Ivanhoe prosper have disappeared. There were pay cuts at the mines, the railroad left that part, and the town was dry of any work. Sinkholes have also been rampant in the area, swallowing roads and whole houses in a single night.

Knocking the dust off one's shoes or washing the feet is decreed by God's word and, as I've been taught, should only be done in dire circumstances. Here it seems Sheffey was directed in his actions, since in his eyes the town was a pit headed for hell. However, the descendants of Ivanhoe still suffer for it though they are good folks, at least the ones I've met.

PEGGY BUCK CLAWSON

A story I found while writing this book actually involves one of my ancestors, Peggy Clawson, a melungeon woman and my fourth great-grandmother. The family story goes that she was really mean and dominating over her husband, William. Instead of folks saying she was the wife of William, she'd rather have it as he is the husband of Peggy. Born in November of 1778, she lived in what was then Watauga County, North Carolina, now the border between Ashe and Wilkes counties.

They say one day she was going to church and stopped at a water hole off Big Ivy Road when she saw a bear come down to the water. She decided to hop into a small boat, paddled over to the bear, and held his head underwater with the paddle until he drowned. Then she paddled the boat back, and walked down the ridge to attend Sunday church. That water hole is now called the Peggy Hole, but local lore gives a different reason behind the name.

In the present day, there is a local legend about that water hole and a witch named Peggy Buck. The story goes that some man took up with a melungeon woman and she became pregnant. Back in those days, melungeon people were considered mongrels and nobody would "harbor" one. So the story goes that, like many of our people, she took to the ridges and woods to live and have her bastard child. When she gave birth, she was faring okay until her milk began to dry up and the baby began to starve. Having no skills in hunting, and plants not having the substantial nutrients the child needed, she conjured up the Devil who came out of the ground forming the Peggy Hole. She made a deal with him for her child to have enough food, but the Devil tricked her and the child grew teeth and sharp ears and extra fingers (a play it seems on old melungeon stereotypes where melungeons took the place of the boogeyman, folks telling their kids to be good or the melungeons would take them away to their caves).

After this, Peggy swore she'd kill the Devil if she ever met paths with him again. Over time, in order to survive, the legend says she "learned herself to witch" so she could turn into different animals and hunt. One day, her and the babe were at the Peggy Hole and buck came up to the water to drink. Much like the bear in the family story, she drowned it by grabbing its antlers and holding its head under the water, thus the meaning behind "Buck" in her name.

Today it's said that if you say her name three times while passing by the hole, different animals (usually a groundhog, rabbit, and deer) will come out of the forest and run out in front of your car each time in an attempt to wreck you.

DOC MULLINS

One conjure man working on South Central Street in Knoxville was Doc Mullins. Back in those days, the street was filled with merchants who often shared places of business through front doors, alley doors, or even second floor balconies—and it was no different with Doc Mullins, who worked out of a small second shop in the same building as an eating house for African Americans, owned by Blaine and Pearl McGhee at 318 South Central Street.

What little we know of Doc Mullins comes from Bert Vincent in his Strolling column. Records indicate his first name was either Ralph or Richard, and he was said to be in his late forties or early fifties at the time these stories and events took place. In that time, if a person was African American, they identified that fact in news articles. But Vincent neglects this fact in the majority of his stories about Mullins, only mentioning he was "colored" a couple times. Leaving that fact out back in those days led to the belief that the person was white. We also aren't sure when he was born or when he died, as his death certificate contains no date of birth and the tales of his death vary as the decades go by. Different sources point to him being from either Alabama or New Orleans. It's possible he migrated during the yellow fever scare.

Vincent described Doc Mullins' shop as small, with piles of herbs and roots on the floors and hanging on the walls. His usual greeting to folks was, "I'm Doctor Mullins and I'm guaranteed," usually with a bow. Mullins shared secrets with Vincent over the course of their time together, always keeping quiet lest evil spirits hear him. Other times, he denied conjuring altogether, saying folks were fools to believe him. But then the next second he would be paranoid again of haints and spirits listening in on their conversations.

According to Vincent, Doc always carried a personal poke or mojo bag on him to protect against fire, flood, wind, and lightning, as well as weapons such as knives and bullets. Doc Mullins claimed the bag contained powdered lizard tongues, hair from a woman's head, Jimsonweed, and bo' hog root (lovage). Doc Mullins was not only an herb man but a conjurer, too. Looking at the contents of the bag, we can see why it was set for protection against these many things. Have you ever heard of a lizard getting struck by lightning? No. They're also quick to find safety in times of flood and fire. Hair from a woman's head is used a lot in southern Appalachia based on biblical beliefs and observation: Papaw said the only thing he was afraid of besides God was womankind, because she could bleed for a week straight without dying. That same strength may have been called on in the bag. Jimsonweed, also called devil's snare or thorn apple, is an invasive plant, meaning it can endure a lot of environments; finally, bo' hog root may have been used because the plant stands sturdy and straight up, tall and prideful.

GRANNY HACKEL

Another local witch woman named Granny Hackel lived in what is now the Turkeytown community of Carter County's Eighth District in Tennessee. Stories about her and the ridge she lived on—now unofficially named Granny Hackel Ridge, between Watauga and Smalling roads—have circulated for years. She is said to have arrived in the Watauga, Tennessee, area in the 1700s, riding on a black stallion and accompanied by two men. They came across the ridge and Granny pointed to a flat piece of land beneath some towering oaks at the crest, and that is where the men built a cabin for her.

Both men died from unknown causes soon after, but Granny continued her work in the community doctoring those in need, helping the ill with her spells and herbs, and delivering babies. The strange thing with Granny Hackel was that she was never called when a woman "went to straw" to give birth; she just somehow knew and showed up to be of help. Children were her specialty, and folks claim she was so good at her work that she could heal a wound just by looking at it.

Her presence and power were well known, the oddly strong winds on the ridge to this day mean many do not need air conditioning during the summer—just an open window or screen door will do the job. But at the top of the ridge is where the strange nature of the winds can be felt and heard, as it sounds like a church choir singing gospels up near the top. Dowsers have found remains of cabins, springhouses, a church, and a cemetery on the ridge.

WITCHDOCTOR SAM EVANS

Sam Evans was a self-appointed witchdoctor of the Great Smokies. I assume he traveled all up and down this range, as most did, but this story brings him to the area of Big Creek, thirty miles east of Gatlinburg, on the North Carolina side of the border. A family was living in one of the hollers along the creek when their cow started giving off bloody milk, a tell-tale sign of witchery. Going by the old saying that "iron lays the Devil," Evans told the folks to take the top of a Dutch oven and put it in the fireplace until it got red-hot, then prod and probe it with a reaping hook. Soon after, the cow's milk cleared up, and the witch herself sought Evans out to pick a bone with him. During the confrontation, the witch's dress got pulled up, revealing marks all over her legs that resembled those of a reaping hook.

So we can see how varied and multiple these tales are and the colorful array of spiritualism and religion they exemplify. We had met yarb doctors who also conjured, seers who simply hear God speaking about pivotal points in history, witches who made deals with Devils and witchdoctors who took them out. This array of mystic workers includes people of color and those of European descent.

Having been so close in the mountains for centuries, practices melded and mixed almost beyond recognition. In this way, superstitions, usually handed down from mothers to their children during their time at home, often blended. Voodoo charms and European charms likewise melded, as the men freely shared tricks among other folks, where the ingredients were interchanged or replaced by whatever was readily available, such as the luck acquired from carrying the right front paw of a possum, as opposed to the gator foot in New Orleans. The supernatural worldviews of all, as well as the stories, melded into some greater entity that lives on today, hovering over the hills in the form of purple hues and blue smoke. As we dig deeper into the conjuring past of southern Appalachia, we will meet old friends and new ones—and possibly some dangers as well, because this path is filled with briars and laurel hells.

4

CORN AND QUARTERS

You're in for a long run if you consider this work. Having visions and sharing prophecies, prescribing herbal medicines to people and animals, or leading a congregation in a prayer of faith healing doesn't take nearly as much out of you as conjure and root work do. Before you do any kind of work, you need to prepare a few things and practice some new habits.

PRECAUTION RITUALS

You always want to cover your head when doing any kind of work, because you're at a veil or ridge to the otherworld and time runs differently there. Without a covering, your hair will turn gray; you may become forgetful or anxious; you might have insomnia; and any preexisting conditions you may have, such as high blood pressure, arthritis, even heart disease, may worsen. It's not the presence of God or the spirits exactly, but the way of "praying" that conjuring takes. It takes a back-alley door to the other side, and it's not always 100 percent safe. Notice how in many of the previous stories folks seemed a bit crazy in their later years? Not all of them were known to cover their heads. Root work is fine because you're not crossing realms or calling out into them like you are with conjure. It's when spirit is brought into the work that caution is needed.

I was taught to follow these practices when working roots or working with the spirits. You may be an experienced worker from another tradition that calls for something different; that's fine, go by your own ways. But with Appalachian folk magic and the methods and beliefs of practice that make up the body of it, what follows is what is called for.

First, take a piece of red ribbon and sew it into the inner side of each shoe. This will help keep spiritual attachments off you.

Find a hat or head covering that is comfortable for you. (I personally switch between either a toboggan or bandanna, sometimes a ball cap.) This will not only keep your mind from getting away from you or your hair going gray, but it'll also protect you from haints hopping on your back.

It is also recommended that you have a strong, unwavering will and a cunning mind for this work; it's not for the meek. Use your common sense with everything you do and anything that happens. Let your humility be the only tamper on your will. Look folks directly in the eye when speaking to them. A lot can be learned about a person just by looking them in the eyes. It's hard for them to lie to you with that.

Take time to sit in silence a few times a week to keep your mind clear. This work can run you mad if you let it. It'll have your mind every which way, leading to paranoia and fear. You will not be invincible, nor all powerful. You will be capable: beyond that is God and the spirits. This is also recommended in order to listen to the spirits, but you must be silent. In these times of quiet, I read a chapter of the Bible repeatedly. I also recommend any of David's Psalms.

Keep a good amount of privacy for yourself. The more folks know about you or your plans, the more you "show your belly" and make yourself vulnerable to the evil eye, the most common curse. To guard against this, and bring luck, wear your left sock inside out. And wear a silver dime around your ankle or neck to protect from conjuring.

Tie your shoes from left to right to keep you standing well. Don't drag or scuff your feet when you walk; that'll kick obstacles into your own path, as Aunt Nelly used to say.

Listen more than you speak. Set time aside for yourself to rest and heal. (My family never works on Sundays, except for on personal things.) And always think ahead. Take care of your body if you plan on doing faith healing—you need to be sure that any pains or symptoms you experience are "phantom pains" from working on a person and not something in your own body. For this and conjure work, prescribe yourself a monthly non-lather bath. (We'll look more at cleansing in a bit.)

Never leave used napkins or disposable drinks around people you don't trust. I take my trash home with me; I don't even toss out a cigarette butt. Same goes for hair and nails: keep them in a safe place or burn them to make sure no one else gets their hands on them.

Just about everyone has their own jack or personal charm they carry with them that protects the holder from all harm and danger, physical or spiritual.

Most importantly, find balance in your life, and always keep your home protected. It is your nest, and nothing else should set up shelter there.

SIGNS AND OMENS

Before doing any kind of work, the general rule is to watch for signs and omens, controlled and non-controlled, regarding a situation. We take these as messages from God and the spirits, and most folks do this for simple and mundane things. There's a farm off the side of the road I take going to work in the morning that is home to about five donkeys, including a solid white one. I always make it a point to notice which direction they're facing and where on the hill they are.

Since we've been isolated in these mountains for centuries, we know the pattern of these hills, the migration of the birds, the habits of the land animals and fish. We have also set a code to each unusual or special behavior they exhibit: if you see cows scratching themselves against farm equipment in the morning, you're going to receive some long-awaited news; if a cat washes its face with its back turned toward the fireplace or front door, it'll rain soon; these are non-controlled signs, events that cannot be affected by humans.

Controlled signs border on root work, as they are actions taken by someone, usually of unnatural origin, to effect a certain result. A couple examples are carrying a walnut to cure rheumatism or washing your hair in stump water to make it long and thick. We create the same in root work and watch for such signs on setting out to do a job. If heading to get medicine for a person or animal, the roots of the plant are examined: if they are gnarly and knotted, it's a bad sign; but if they are straight and strong, it's favorable.

Hearing or seeing certain birds upon starting can also be indications of the path ahead. For example, if you see a turkey vulture circling, and you're heading to cure an illness, it's not likely to work. However, these signs are treated in context. So if you're heading somewhere to lay a curse or get herbs for the same and you see a turkey vulture, it is a good sign.

If a rabbit crosses your path during a work, regardless of the type, its direction should be noted: if it crosses left to right, expect success; if it crosses right to left, it's not likely to work. If you see a cat, note the path it takes: if it comes up from behind you, Spirit backs you in the work. If it walks toward you, expect some opposition or obstacles. If it crosses your path, its direction foretells the same as the rabbit above. However, orange or calico cats are signs of sure success. If ants are crawling in your pathway going in a set direction, that is good, but if they are aimlessly walking around, go back and try the next day or set course for another action.

Now, we can't always just sit and wait for signs. Sometimes you won't see a bird or anything in your walks. This is why controlled omens have been harnessed through different forms of divination. Nobody here I know ever calls it divination, by the way. They just pull out cards or bones or a bowl of water, usually saying something like, "Let's see" or "I bet." All three of the following methods have little recording in the past here, but just about everyone knows of someone who's done these things. Before practicing any kind of divination, you'll want to pray by the three highest names—because anything can be lurking about wanting to have a quick "chat." Just as you wouldn't want to have a conversation with the creepy person at the gas station at 3 A.M., keep that same energy when speaking to spirits.

Remember, even the Devil can recite Scripture—and he can lead you to believe it, too, which is why we never read for ourselves. Mama will read for me and I'll read for her, because the sty in the eye can get in the way: you'll see and read what you want to instead of what you *need* to. Even then, there are times when I will cut my own cards and then send my mother a picture for interpretation, and she does the same, if we're not able to be under the same roof.

Remember to keep your head covered. If you're in your own home and you have it set right against unknown spirits, then you're fine without the covering.

Never do readings where you sleep, either, so you don't get woken up in the middle of the night. My mother has always slept on the couch. She wanted us to each have our own room growing up, and a bed hurts her back. So, since she sometimes read cards on the couch, she would give it a light dusting of baby powder afterward and wash her hair to get rid of any spiritual attachments or "ick" left behind—especially if she read for someone who wasn't blood.

SWITCHING

Probably the most widely known form of divination—or spelling, as the old folks called it—is switching or water witching. Witching sticks would be used to lead a person to water, to treasures such as gold, or even the direction a person is in. Melungeons were often said to be excellent dowsers because they always found a gold or silver mine on their ridges, which they used to make counterfeit money, containing more precious metals than the government's currency. In the 1960s, dowsing rods were also used by the United States military to find mines, tunnels, hidden camps, and other things. They can also be used to find roots that have been planted on your property. According to tradition, the stick should be cut from a stone fruit tree, like peach, apple, plum, or dogwood. Some folks say you can also use willow or any wood that is flexible, but peach and apple seem to be the most common. In Appalachia, it's said there's a water witch in every generation of the family, but the youngest can't witch for water until the oldest has passed. There can only be one active water witch at a time. Some folks are never able to take up the sticks. It can make them sick, give them headaches, and cause a whole range of issues if they don't have the knack for it, but it never hurts to try.

Some folks said simple prayers while looking for water, using Bibles suspended on strings tied to house keys, with the string being placed in the book at the following verse and then hung on a forked branch driven into the ground, which would bend and sway if there was water beneath. Others simply prayed the verse Psalm 78:15–16:

> 15 *He clave the rocks in the wilderness, and gave them*
> *drink as out of the great depths.*
> 16 *He brought streams also out of the rock, and caused*
> *waters to run down like rivers.*

Witching sticks take on a few forms throughout the South. In southern Appalachia, it is the forked branch in a Y shape, with the leg of the Y being the smallest section. The two prongs of the Y are gripped, palms up, and held aloft at the base of the ribs with the leg of the Y pointing out and up a little bit. Keep the thumbs extended, with your palms at least 4 inches from the end of each prong. The stick should be cut about 4 to 6 inches behind the fork or where the prongs join together. Then cut the prongs to the same length, ideally between 10 and 14 inches.

The stick will indicate that water or whatever you're seeking is below by pulling or dipping downward or upward (it varies from person to person). The movement will be barely noticeable at first, but the closer you get, the stronger the pull will be. I heard a story of one man who didn't believe in such stuff, so he gave it a try. The stick pulled. Then it pulled again. He thought he'd outsmart it and everyone there, so he made the tightest grip he could on the prongs. Well, he stepped right over where the water was, and the stick pulled downward with such force it peeled the bark off where his hands were and snapped one of the prongs! Don't underestimate this stuff. If you're just starting out, the stick may pull even if you're just near the thing and not right over it. This is because you have to get used to being this channel, and the more you practice dowsing, the more on the mark you will be.

The second form of witching stick, often called a bobbing stick, is a long branch that is thicker on one end than the other. The thinner end can be held in the right or left hand, depending on who you ask, between the thumb and the two first fingers; the thickest part is left to dangle outward, bowing the branch a bit with its weight. The bobbing stick's meaning differs from the Y-shaped dowsing rod's. Once over water or near what you are looking for, the stick is said to bob or shake, meaning its bowed middle will vibrate. The stronger it gets, the closer you are. Held outward by the forefinger and thumb with the end resting against your palm, the stick should be about 20 inches long, and freshly cut. Usually bobbing sticks are used to determine the number of things, specifically the depth you'll have to dig to reach water, in which case the unit of measurement is either 1 foot or 10 feet per bob, depending on who you ask. It was often used after the pronged stick had identified the location. Count the number of vertical vibrations, and when the stick is finished, it will shake horizontally.

If you have the Gift and wish to continue using the same stick, depending on the wood and how long it's dried, you may be able to soak it in hot water overnight to make it flexible again. Nowadays, folks will also use L-shaped wire rods that are held in each hand at the shorter length. When they cross, that's the spot or a yes; if they point away from each other, it's a no; if they don't cross but point in a direction, head to that spot. They are usually 12 to 18 inches on the top part and the handle is generally 4 to 6 inches long and wrapped in plastic tubing. The handles of mine are made with straws cut to size. They can be made from wire bought at a craft store or made from old wire coat hangers. I've even heard of some folks using a coat hanger in its original form to dowse and witch for things, simply holding it at the corners with the hook facing out and up.

And some folks don't use tools at all—only their hands! Called hand tremblers, they walk around with their hands open, palms facing the ground, while shaking them like jazz hands. Once they are at the point of water or whatever they're looking for, a number of things happen: their hands stop shaking by themselves, they get warm or cold, or a feeling of needles comes to the hands and fingers.

Still yet, some folks carry the thing they are looking for on them, whether it's a small bottle of water, or a piece of coal, gold, or copper. After determining the depth of the water, for example, you can use different types of rock to determine what needs to be drilled through in order to get to the water source.

If you do decide to keep a stick to use and simply reanimate it with hot water overnight, do so while praying to the spirits to help you find whatever you're looking for. When you're not using the stick, wrap it up in a white cloth and store it somewhere dry. I'd recommend replacing your witching sticks every year, hunting them in the early spring or summer, when the wood is new, and burning them in the winter.

Whatever type of tool you decide to try, test it out by walking your own property trying to find the water pipe that leads to your home. You might have wonderful luck the first time, or you might have to try a few times to see if the stick or rod will work for you. Keep a clear mind and focus on what it is you're after. You may also need to take breaks, as dowsing requires a good bit of concentration and muscle, and can be draining physically and spiritually. If dowsing gives you a headache, makes you nauseous, or gives you the shakes, it may not be for you.

Another tool in this practice is the plumb bob, which is a weighted object suspended by a thread whose movements indicate directions or yes/no responses. It's essentially a pendulum. A plumb bob was also used to find lost objects and even people, as in the murder case of Frances Silver in 1833. "Frankie" Silver was accused and hung on the crime of killing her husband, Charlie Silver. That morning, Charlie had chopped a week's worth of wood. Frankie told folks she suspected him of seeing another woman on these "hunting" trips of his; that's why he chopped so much wood—because he planned to be gone for a while. She made the first chop as he slept on the couch and the final one after he got up and fell to the floor.

She used the week's worth of wood to burn his body in the fireplace and hid those things that wouldn't burn, such as his belt buckle, metal buttons, and teeth, all over the property, under floorboards, and in tree stumps. He had been missing for a while when folks began noticing his absence, backed by Frankie's claims of him hunting, but all that wood he had chopped was gone. Charlie's father, John, worried about his boy, traveled over the mountains from Burke County to a farm about forty miles away in Zionville, Tennessee, to request aid from a slave owner whose slave, Jonas, had a knack for finding folks. Jonas wasn't there, though, so Williams, the owner, did it for him. He told John to draw a map of mountains and creeks and things that Charlie may have crossed on his trip. Williams tied the string to a rafter, pulled it back, and released it over the map. The plumb bob spun and swung for a while and then stopped like the needle of a compass right over where Charlie's home was. Williams, thinking it didn't work, pulled the string—but the plumb bob held its position over the square.

You can make a plumb bob from anything—a ring, a holed bullet, a holed quarter, a stone, a piece of broken plate. The string it is suspended from should be about the length from your hind knuckles to the inner bend of your arm. Hold the string between the thumb and index finger. Arch your hand and wrist up a bit, and hold it a good distance from yourself, keeping the hand at chest level. Establish your answers by asking it what yes is and what no is. It will swing clockwise, counterclockwise, side to side, or back and forth. These change depending on the person and can even change from time to time, so always ask it what yes or no is first.

To fine-tune the plumb bob, wind the string around a stick until the weight is 2 inches below. Take a sample of something you're looking for, such as money, aluminum, copper, or water, and place it on a table. Slowly unwind the string while holding it over the sample until the plumb bob starts moving at a maximum pace. It is now tuned to find that object.

NUMBERS AND COUNTING

Numbers play an important part in most magical systems, and Appalachian folk magic is no exception. The secrets of numbers have long been discovered in these hills, first through the Bible and then through lucky dream number books sold in pharmacies and trade outlets. Biblically, numbers are the foundation for the measurements of the world.

They measure the days and nights and minutes and hours from the time man took his first shaking steps.

Numbers were used to set the firmament and the Earth alike: Christ had twelve disciples, died with five wounds, and expired in the ninth hour. There are seven Holy Spirits of God, He holds seven stars in his hand, and before His throne is a lamb with seven horns and seven eyes.

The Cherokee baptized children on the fourth day after birth, and they recognized seven directions: up, down, center, north, east, south, and west. Many of their medicines had to be applied four or seven times, with the corresponding song being sung the same number of times. They believed Creation was completed in seven days and they had seven clans.

Growing up, many southerners are warned against counting things without rhyme or reason. If you count the stars, you'll number your own days or years. If you count the teeth of a comb, you'll conjure bad luck to yourself. On the other hand, counting is accomplished for such goals as gaining wishes, in the case of counting one hundred white horses. Warts are counted and the same number of knots are made in string to tie them up and take them off. To cure hiccoughs, count backward from your age with your mouth closed.

Because of this, numbers have had a significant impact on mankind, especially those in the lowest livelihoods. Most folks back in the day were very poor and oftentimes had to drop out of school early to help the family either in the mines, in the timber mills, on the tracks, or on family land. Not everyone had a fair education according to today's standards, so what little they did know helped them in more ways than we can know today—counting money, estimating crop production, managing household income, and rationing—all just to get by. They didn't know much and often couldn't read, but if they could count and help raise a family right, that was all the blessing they needed.

I mentioned before the distinction between controlled and uncontrolled signs. With the distinctive nature of our relationship with Creation in the mountains, it's no wonder folks often looked outside the pages of the Good Book to find answers through the things that knew God first: the plants and animals, our eldest siblings. Growths and bends and odd appearances in nature were often interpreted in many ways, whether it was how low the wasps nested, how early the squirrels started foraging for nuts, how thick or thin an animal's fur was, or how many leaves or petals a randomly picked herb had; they all had a tale to tell.

Counting Corn

If you have a question, pray Psalm 23 twenty-three times before finding a corncob, either in your garden or at your local grocery:

> 1 *The Lord is my shepherd; I shall not want.*
>
> 2 *He maketh me to lie down in green pastures: he leadeth me beside the still waters.*
>
> 3 *He restoreth my soul: he leadeth me in the paths of righteousness for his name's sake.*
>
> 4 *Yea, though I walk through the valley of the shadow of death, I will fear no evil: for thou art with me; thy rod and thy staff they comfort me.*
>
> 5 *Thou preparest a table before me in the presence of mine enemies: thou anointest my head with oil; my cup runneth over.*
>
> 6 *Surely goodness and mercy shall follow me all the days of my life: and I will dwell in the house of the Lord for ever.*

GARDEN METHOD

Walk around the garden counterclockwise while spelling your full name (first, middle, and last) and stop at the row of corn when you speak the last letter of your name. When you've made it there, count down to the respective number of stalks to your left. Each number has the following significance:

One: For questions relating to spirituality, God, and faith.

Two: For love and any kind of partnerships or agreements.

Three: For general inquiries on the present condition of situations or people, like how things are going.

Four: In regards to travel and inquiries of things happening from afar or to people far away.

Five: For questioning safety and the well-being of oneself, especially in matters of possible witchcraft.

Six: For health inquiries.

Seven: For inquires on luck and money.

Eight: To find out the result of a proposal, such as future plans of any sort.

Pick the highest cob on that stalk and pay attention to how long it takes you to pull it off, as you can only use your hands. If there's a lot of resistance, the answer to your question is no. If it's easy or quite quick, it's a yes.

Pull back the fodder and rip it off. Look to the foremost row of kernels facing you and count to the right, that row being one. Mark it by pulling one of the kernels out so you know where you began. If the number is odd, it is bad/no. If it is even, it is good/yes. Finally, take into account any blights it may have. Are there holes in the kernels?

If so, that is bad. If all is well with the kernels overall, look to their orientation. Are the rows straight? That is good and no difficulty or obstacles are foreseen. If the rows are crooked, there will be difficulties or disagreements. If there are kernels missing naturally, the number missing is the number for your solution.

Now put this all together. Say your question is, "Is Billy Bob running around on me?" The cob is fairly easy to pull and doesn't take long, but it's kind of tough as well. There are twenty-four rows of kernels. There are a few holes in the kernels, but they rest in straight rows. Three kernels are naturally missing. This would tell me that, based on the harvesting, something is up firsthand. We have an even twenty-four rows, which means yes. However, twenty-four is a balanced number, and half of it is twelve. This number we can estimate a time such as twelve months ago or in the last twelve months the situation occurred. Further, we have a few holes, but they're not so bad you can't still eat it; and the kernels rest in straight rows, so no difficulties. I would assume both parties are at fault and that Billy Bob was ashamed and came to his senses. Considering the number of holes in the kernels, he didn't let it get too far and soon got back on the "straight path." The three missing kernels can be applied to magical and non-magical solutions. Since the events have passed and Billy Bob is already ashamed, I would be sure to have three good moments with him to remind him of love.

Magically, we could also take up Billy Bob's left footprint each day for three days. If it's in dirt, scoop it up with a spoon going from the toe to the heel. If it is on concrete, take a wet washcloth and wipe in the same manner from toe to heel. Mark the location of the footprint with a stone or even a piece of mulch, and put these to work before the next rain, or it'll wash his steps away and the root will take longer to find him (when he returns home again). Take the print and put it in a plastic sandwich bag with a bit of your urine while calling his name and telling him to stay faithful and to remember why he loves you. Place this beneath your underwear in a drawer or chest.

GROCERY METHOD

Go to your local supermarket and spell your full name silently to yourself, finishing as you arrive at the corn. For this, cobs still in their husks are ideal. Count from left to right the respective number for what you wish to know, as shown above. Once you've chosen your ear of corn, notice its husk. If it is in fair condition, with one hole or less, it is a good and fair sign. If the husk is dead or brown in places with many holes, it wavers toward the bad or negative.

Pull back the fodder and rip it off. Look to the foremost row of kernels facing toward you and count to the right, that row being one. Mark it by pulling one of the kernels out so you know where you began. If the number is odd, it is bad/no. If it is even, it is good/yes. Finally, take into account any blights it may have. Are there holes in the kernels? If so, that is bad. If all is well with the kernels overall, look to their orientation. Are the rows straight? That is good and no difficulty or obstacles are foreseen. If the rows are crooked, there will be difficulties or disagreements. If there are kernels missing naturally, that is a number for your solution.

To use this as a work, it would depend on the situation. If you're wondering about protection for yourself or another and the reading is not favorable, cut off both ends of the cob and bake them for an hour at 150 degrees—just be careful not to burn them. Once dried, write your name on the inner side of each, first name on one and last name on the other. Tie these together (flat sides facing each other) and carry them with you wrapped in a piece of blue flannel. Blue flannel was traditional back in the day among conjure workers. While the lay folks made charms out of whatever fabric they had, blue flannel was often used for protection and red flannel was reserved for other works, such as money and love.

THROWING THE BONES

I have personally been throwing the bones for eleven years now and was taught by a family friend named Gracie. She often babysat us when we were little while Mama worked. She was a warm-hearted woman; she'd give you the shirt off her back if you needed it. She was also odd like us, though. She had fly ribbons in every room in her house, although I only saw maybe one fly in all the times I was there. "Keeps the bad stuff from gettin' to ya," she once said. I assumed the bad stuff was the flies, but now I know different.

The day she taught me was sometime in the fall of 2007 and Mama was running late for work. On the couch was a small box with six chicken bones in it. After we had been there a little while, she tossed them on the floor and told us not to touch them, and she sat there staring at them like they were going to do something. I asked what she was doing. She looked at me for a bit and said, "I'm talking with them."

"How?" I asked. "I don't hear anything."

She said, "I could tell you how it's done, but only once—and if you don't remember, then the bones won't talk with you."

She picked up a bone and prayed over it. She named it Birth. She picked up another bone and did the same thing. Its name was Love and Hate. The hate part was the smaller end of the bone, with darker cartilage.

"Do this with all of them," she said, "naming every part of life for them. Then you go wash them in the creek and set them somewhere dark for three days. After that, they'll tell you the secrets they know once they're thrown. The talking ones shake when they speak."

That was it. That was all she showed me. After that, I was on my own.

Beyond a physical teacher, once their job is done, the bones take over and teach you the rest at your own pace, where you're able to truly listen to them, until you get to the point where spiritual "listening" is second nature. You know exactly what they're saying and why, which bones are "shaking," and for what.

When I first began reading the bones, a few years after Gracie passed away, I remembered what she said upon receiving a gift of possum bones from a friend. I expected the bones to actually shake. I won't say what they did, but if they'll talk to you, you'll soon understand the meaning behind those words. They do talk, though, and they've never lied to me.

Bone throwing in America largely originated in Africa, and it seems the practice is more common the farther south you go, considering this was outside the main "Baptist" territory where anything African Americans did was deemed Devil worship, accounting for the large lack of African elements in the Appalachian folk magic system aside from foot track magic and some other things.

The composition of your bone set is personal. I know some readers who have upward of sixty bones in their set, while others only retain a specific number or even just as many as they can hold in their cupped hands. I try to keep with the latter, because Gracie only had six bones. My set now has about thirty bones, the largest being 4 inches long, and I can hold all of them in my cupped hands. The common (and some would say traditional) bones used are raccoon, possum, and chicken. However, some people include other things such as dried alligator feet, coyote teeth, and even chicken feet. Starr Casas gives a wonderful explanation of different bones and their possible meanings in her book *Divination Conjure Style*. In my set, I have a small alligator foot I got on a visit to Cherokee, North Carolina, a snake rib, and a coyote tooth with one end blackened with a marker, which denotes arguments and hostility.

In setting the meanings, some folks like Starr go by the behavior of the animal or the characteristics of the particular part. For example, a leg bone could symbolize movement; a wing bone could signify change

or a swiftness in events. I sometimes use this method in naming the
bones, but usually I will sit with a particular bone and simply name it,
telling my ancestors and spirits as well, or I will let them tell me. They've
sometimes told me what a particular bone should be in dreams.

Traditionally, your bones should be found, either in full skeletal form and broken down and processed, in the case of a chicken
or possum used as food, or simply accumulated over time. However,
in today's age, when the number of hunters is at its lowest ever, it is
possible to purchase them. In doing so, I strongly recommend buying from folks with a good reputation in the taxidermy community
who sell bones acquired through an animal's natural death or from
one raised for food by a small farm. Roadkill bones, in my experience,
take a very long time to speak because of the animal's traumatic death.
Avoid these as best you can, but if that is all that is available to you,
place those (cleaned) bones in a box of cedar, tobacco, and cornmeal.
Pray Psalm 23 over it three times a day for seven days (see page 66),
offering prayers of peace to the animal's spirit. If you still find reading
with these bones difficult, it would be best to bury them and acquire
others. Not every animal spirit gives up its bones easy, and that's okay.

You can store your set in a box or bag. I use an old burlap bag for
mine, but prior to that I used a Crown Royal bag. Take the set to a
creek or river and wash it in a low tide area. (You don't want to lose
any of the bones in the tide.) Because of my close connection with my
bones, I wash them one by one and repeat this process every spring
or whenever I feel they are tired and "feeding" them won't help. After
washing the bones, I revive them by prayer, specifically by praying Ezekiel 37:1–9 over them and breathing into them four times:

> 1 The hand of the Lord was upon me, and carried me
> out in the spirit of the Lord, and set me down in the
> midst of the valley which was full of bones,

2 And caused me to pass by them round about: and, behold, there were very many in the open valley; and, lo, they were very dry.

3 And he said unto me, Son of man, can these bones live? And I answered, O Lord God, thou knowest.

4 Again he said unto me, Prophesy upon these bones, and say unto them, O ye dry bones, hear the word of the Lord.

5 Thus saith the Lord God unto these bones; Behold, I will cause breath to enter into you, and ye shall live:

6 And I will lay sinews upon you, and will bring up flesh upon you, and cover you with skin, and put breath in you, and ye shall live; and ye shall know that I am the Lord.

7 So I prophesied as I was commanded: and as I prophesied, there was a noise, and behold a shaking, and the bones came together, bone to his bone.

8 And when I beheld, lo, the sinews and the flesh came up upon them, and the skin covered them above: but there was no breath in them.

9 Then said he unto me, Prophesy unto the wind, prophesy, son of man, and say to the wind, Thus saith the Lord God; Come from the four winds, O breath, and breathe upon these slain, that they may live.

I then pray one of these verses over them three times:

For nothing is secret, that shall not be made manifest; neither any thing hid, that shall not be known and come abroad (Luke 8:17).

*Therefore whatsoever ye have spoken in darkness shall
be heard in the light; and that which ye have spoken in
the ear in closets shall be proclaimed upon the housetops
(Luke 12:3).*

These verses serve to open the cradles, hearts, and graves of man to reveal all things in the light and in the dark. The bones are no simple tool; they give secrets freely and have no respect for persons. In my years of reading them, the bones know no difference between a rich man and a poor one. Our hearts are all the same, and the bones are our shared end result.

Your bones should be fed monthly during the full moon and after every reading. It is best to cleanse them first of the other person's energies with a strong liquor (never let anyone else touch them, of course). I will sprinkle a few drops of moonshine on the bones. After this, I feed them by sprinkling whiskey over them and giving them blows of tobacco smoke.

Keep your bones in their bag or box when you're not using them.

Most folks dedicate their bones to their ancestors and keep them on their ancestor altar as well to further empower and protect them.

I've found that when you're just starting out, it's best to use only a couple bones to see if they speak to you or to see if you're able to tell what they're trying to say. If you have trouble distinguishing the bones from each other, you can tie colored strings around them or mark them with lines, dots, or crosses using a marker. Generally, you also want to have bones between 2 and 6 inches long. Anything bigger and heavier is likely to weaken and eventually break smaller bones in your set. To avoid this, never toss the bones on very hard surfaces, such as tile or concrete. You can use carpeted floors, wood floors, or the ground outside. Bone reading, as I was taught and shown, is done on the floor. However, I know some folks (not in the Appalachian tradition) who use tabletops for casting, which I have done before as well, on an end table, when my back wasn't feeling up to sitting on the floor.

To keep the bones from bouncing and knocking around a lot, I also recommend tossing them on a throwing cloth. Gracie didn't use one, but I do. In the end it's up to you if you have the Gift and can speak with them. I use a white bandanna. Other folks use animal skins, but in my experience it is very hard to find one that lays completely flat, which could affect the throw.

When you begin, sit and clear your mind. Here you can invite your spirits in or simply focus on your question or the matter at hand. At this point I pray the Prayer of Daniel (Daniel 2:20–23):

> *20 Blessed be the name of God for ever and ever: for wisdom and might are his:*
>
> *21 And he changeth the times and the seasons: he removeth kings, and setteth up kings: he giveth wisdom unto the wise, and knowledge to them that know understanding:*
>
> *22 He revealeth the deep and secret things: he knoweth what is in the darkness, and the light dwelleth with him.*
>
> *23 I thank thee, and praise thee, O thou God of my fathers, who hast given me wisdom and might, and hast made known unto me now what we desired of thee: for thou hast now made known unto us the king's matter. (I replace "the king's matter" with "all matters.")*

As you get further into concentration, gently shake the bag about a foot off the floor, then empty it quickly when you feel they have their message ready. Once the bones have fallen, begin studying them. Bones running parallel either show movement or a path. Bones that cross affect the others' meaning, depending on which is on the top or bottom.

Generally, you always want a starting point, so you need a bone that represents you (or whoever you're reading for). From this you can see the influence the other bones have toward you. You may also simply lay something of yours down and cast on that, such as an earring, a ring, or a key, to represent yourself in the reading. If you are reading for someone, you can even use a small slip of paper with the person's name and birthday written on it in a pinch.

1. *Person Bone (You)*; 2. *Enemy Bone*; 3. *Conflict/Peace*; 4. *Wishes/Plans*; 5. *Strength/Health*; 6. *Burdens/Stress/Worry*; 7. *Construction/Main Problem*

In the figure shown above, we see an example of a bone throw. We have a bone representing you (1), one representing opposing forces (2), conflict or peace (3), and so on. With the claw, conflict here would be indicated by where the end of the claw points. If it points away, there's no conflict; however, here it does show issue since it points toward the first bone. The first bone covers the enemy bone, where the conflict shown by bone 3 resides, meaning you or the person you're reading for will overcome the issue, but in doing so they may undermine their own wishes or goals (bone 4). Bones 5 and 6 show this has put some stress on the person. It doesn't look like this has been going on for long, because these bones are fairly close to bone 1. The seventh bone shows constriction, restraint, or whatever is holding one back. This bone is far from the enemy but close to the worry and stress, showing that the enemy isn't the one holding the person back—it's the worry and fear of that opposing person or force—and because of this, they are hurting themselves and undermining their strength. In such a situation, I would assure the person that they will overcome the obstacles, and possibly without sacrificing one bit of their wishes or plans. What they need to handle is their self-esteem, their own self-worth, and they need to acknowledge their strength. Without doing so, they would become their own obstacle.

Let's say bone 2 was a love bone. That's all we are changing, but it would change the entire meaning of the throw. This is why it can take years to truly learn the bones. They'll switch up on you without question on the spot. (You'll learn what I mean by that if you're meant to talk with them.) So in this new case, the bones tell us that the person has crossed their lover somehow, thus causing fights and arguments. I would say they crossed them or created the issue because it is their bone that crosses the love bone. Here, the wishbone or bone 4 would take on a slightly different position: the basis for the fight seems to be a disagreement in emotions. The person isn't sure what they want for the future, and these emotions are conflicting with the lover's thoughts and plans for them both. The other bones still have their same meanings of stress, worry, and constriction. Trouble in love often seeps into every aspect of life. It is in our nature to desire a companion, and when there are issues with this, it negatively affects the non-natural aspects of our lives, such as work. This in turn affects income, which affects other areas of one's life, and on and on. These bones then, by bone 7, would identify this issue as the cause of other problems arising in the person's life, an issue they haven't dealt with.

Once you set the meanings for the bones, they are still subject to change on a case-by-case basis, but they may change permanently by themselves. The spirit of them will simply feel *different*. Bones act somewhat like the cards—their meanings are relative to the ones around them—so each "name" is general, just like Gracie told me. "Birth" could mean something new, expected, coming soon, or an actual child. "Love and Hate" could encompass emotional ranges, how you feel about something, close or distant, love or pure disdain. My set also contains bones representing money, friends or strangers, a man, a woman, and the spirits.

Although they aren't much, the bones can possess such a spirit and power that you become bonded with them over time. In periods of not using them, you will feel them call to you in dreams or they may even make your own bones ache and pain until you feed them and let them breathe. Because they become an extension of you, always cleanse them after every reading and never let anyone else touch them. Absolutely no one.

The first year or so of reading and interpreting their messages will be hard, but the wisdom the bones hold is endless. But much like the witching sticks, you have to have an innate knack for it. They have to be *willing* to speak with you. So if nothing comes of it, do not force it. A couple of folks I have been willing to teach have continued to try and try to no avail and it negatively affected their health, with daily migraines, nightmares, insomnia, and constant nausea, at which point I advised them to bury the bones in the woods and their troubles stopped. The bones are powerful. As little as six simple chicken bones can embody all aspects and tales of life.

So there you have it, your eyes and ears in this work. These methods will guide you in maneuvering the spiritual and the physical to avoid danger, find solutions to problems, and prepare yourself for coming events. Remember, nothing in the future is set in stone. So take up the deck, the stalks, or the bones, and prepare to work.

In the following chapter, you will meet the many alleys and hidden spaces of conjure in Appalachia. Everything isn't what it seems, and nothing is fully safe or foolproof. This work can affect you physically in many negative ways, likely stemming from any preexisting problems. To prevent worsening these and hurting yourself, we will first look at forms of cleansing and protection. From there we will delve into the recipes for daily life. There are numerous ingredients used for many things, so an organized list can be found in appendix B, sectioned by need or desire.

5

PRAYING AT THE RIVER

I n Appalachian culture, everyone is born with a sense of respon-
sibility for one another, especially those who are kin. We care for
each other in almost every aspect of life. There have been countless
occasions when my elders went hungry to make sure I ate and where
I offset bills to make sure they had groceries. Not favors or loans or
borrows. It is simply how we do things. We take care of each other out
here. No matter what. And that's quite literal. No matter what!

But how should you care for your fellows if you're not well, if
you're sick, physically or spiritually? There are many ways that we
release these burdens from ourselves. Some call it the weight of sin,
others call it bad blood—but to the majority these are all the same
thing and it can be a simultaneously physical and spiritual complaint.
Many folks here believe that demons and spirits and magic and sin can
make you spiritually and physically sick. Eden wasn't just the origin of
evil and sin in the world, but also that of death and disease—they go
hand in hand. "For the wages of sin is death," according to the Scrip-
tures, meaning if you live and act poorly, then you will come to a poor
end result (either illness or death). As it was explained to me growing up, the godly or spiritual life aids in a healthy life spiritually and
physically. Of course, good people do get sick, but likely for mundane

reasons. Other folks, those who sin, come to a life filled with obstacles and illness on many levels.

In conjure this isn't taken by the popular interpretation that sin leads you away from God—that is between each individual and their Maker and is not my business. With this work, it takes on a different meaning: when folks aren't protected properly, they are more vulnerable to a number of things, including spiritual attachments and witchcraft. But of course no one is perfect, which is where the role of the conjurers and witchdoctors come into play. They doctor the spirit. They "doctor the Devil" out of you. Sin is sickness, and sickness is sin to the mountaineers; whatever's out of balance isn't in balance with the Almighty and needs to be adjusted. You may try to cast away as many obstacles and troubles from your life as you can, but if there isn't change in your own habits or behaviors, you'll come to the same rugged paths. That is sin to a conjurer: wishing for a better life but not putting in effective steps to better it. This is where conjure and folk magic help the mountaineer. They are a ladder, a stepping stool out of the metaphorical pit that exists in these hills populated with haints and paranoia, addiction, and struggle. Of course it isn't all foolproof. We are all still subject to a greater will. But we can at least try to better it all.

In Appalachian spirituality and religion, demons and spirits are a very real and palpable presence, with just as much influence as anything else. Stories abound of demons in the woods and creeks, of dead men with spinning heads sitting on boulders, overseeing roads passing beneath, and folks with a wrong twinkle in their eye. Salvation and damnation both rose from these hills; this is their house, and it isn't a peaceful one. The doors slam with drug addiction, the foundation quakes with church revivals, the attic is filled with hollow angels singing songs of judgment, and the basement is a never-ending coal mine filled with knocks for every sin and failure of everyone in the Land of the Forgotten.

The Appalachian landscape has been a frightful terrain since the American frontier, when stories of black panthers were abundant. Today, our fears are more spiritual but no less dangerous. I've told you previously of how fragile the human body and spirit are. The slightest change and we could be brought to our deathbed, led either by disease or the hand of a haint. In doing this work, you need to stay protected. You need to be cleansed and cleansed again. The spirit is just like the body; it gets dirty and needs to shed skin. Sometimes with just general wear and tear, but other times via an attachment or something that got in through the cracks. It is here that spirituality and religion act as the immune system for the soul. So let's build your immune system.

SPIRITUAL BATHING

When you do this work, you want to make sure you are cleansed so nothing gets in the way of your goals. Cleansing by water has been done for thousands of years, and in Appalachia this was often achieved at the river—especially one where baptisms often took place. This is a sort of baptism itself, returning you to your organic self. A reset. We go through life today subconsciously sticking things to ourselves, such as stress and burdens. This weight further weakens you and will lead to haints wishing to follow you home and play with you and your life.

A haint is any spirit with ill intentions, whether it be an ancestor who lived and died badly, a wandering soul, a demon, or something else. The worst haints are those who have been long forgotten at their graves. They get bored sometimes, and you don't want to be their new form of entertainment!

The following cleansing bath will not only send away haints but will also remove the evil eye and any crossings set against you. Because nothing is ever accomplished overnight, cleansing baths are repeated in cycles. The normal recommendation is to take a cleansing bath over the course of either three to nine days in a row or certain days each week, such as every Sunday for three weeks. With cleansing baths, it is best to take them either before the sun rises or as it sets. If this doesn't work for you, you can work with the clock: take the bath as the hand of the clock goes downward from 12 A.M. or P.M. to 6 A.M. or P.M. This is done to send things away, because you are wanting to remove the bad stuff that has accumulated around you.

Back in the day before indoor plumbing, folks would fill a basin of water from the creek, taken up going with the flow of the water. Once this was done, they would either bathe right there from that basin or take it in the house to bathe, depending on the season and the weather. This way you washed with pure living water. After the bath, the basin would be dumped back into the creek or river, sending the bad stuff on its way. Folks also used to use laundry bluing that had been prayed over for a number of days to empower their clothes against ghosts and witches.

General Cleansing Bath

To prepare your cleansing bath, gather the following:

- 1 cup apple cider vinegar
- 1 capful ammonia
- 3 tablespoons new salt bought specifically for this purpose
- Blessed oil

Fill a bathtub with warm water. Once the tub is full, add the apple cider vinegar, ammonia, and salt as you pray Psalm 30 over the bath three times:

> 1 I will extol thee, O LORD; for thou hast lifted me up, and hast not made my foes to rejoice over me.
>
> 2 O LORD my God, I cried unto thee, and thou hast healed me.

3 O LORD, thou hast brought up my soul from the grave: thou hast kept me alive, that I should not go down to the pit.

4 Sing unto the LORD, O ye saints of his, and give thanks at the remembrance of his holiness.

5 For his anger endureth but a moment; in his favour is life: weeping may endure for a night, but joy cometh in the morning.

6 And in my prosperity I said, I shall never be moved.

7 LORD, by thy favour thou hast made my mountain to stand strong: thou didst hide thy face, and I was troubled.

8 I cried to thee, O LORD; and unto the LORD I made supplication.

9 What profit is there in my blood, when I go down to the pit? Shall the dust praise thee? Shall it declare thy truth?

10 Hear, O LORD, and have mercy upon me: LORD, be thou my helper.

11 Thou hast turned for me my mourning into dancing: thou hast put off my sackcloth, and girded me with gladness;

12 To the end that my glory may sing praise to thee, and not be silent. O LORD my God, I will give thanks unto thee for ever.

When taking the bath, recite the psalm again three times as you wash from head to toe in downward strokes only, not back and forth. When you have finished, drain the water, saving a cup or bucket of it for later. Once the rest of the water has drained, without drying off, you can take a normal shower or bath. Afterward, anoint your head, hands, and feet with blessed oil while saying the Lord's Prayer:

> *Our Father who art in heaven, hallowed be Thy name.*
>
> *Thy Kingdom come, Thy will be done*
>
> *On earth as it is in heaven.*
>
> *Give us this day our daily bread and forgive us our trespasses*
>
> *As we forgive those who trespass against us.*
>
> *Lead us not into temptation, but deliver us from evil.*
>
> *For Thine is the Kingdom and the Power and the Glory forever and ever.*
>
> *Amen.*

Blessed oil: To start, pour your oil (olive oil is common in the South, but my mother has used vegetable oil or bacon grease if needed) into a small bottle. Repeat Psalm 23 over it three times a day for nine consecutive days (see page 66). This oil will then be used for protection. You may also use this oil to anoint the doorframes of your home, going from the back to the front of the house, inside to out, while praying the Lord's Prayer.

After anointing yourself, take the cup or bucket of water outside and cast it toward the sun. Return to the home without looking back. If you're working by the clock, go to the western point of your property and cast it to the west, again returning without looking back. To look back shows doubt, but I was taught to never look back for another reason: you may see the Thing, and that can make you vulnerable to it again.

For twenty-four to forty-eight hours after the bath, avoid crowded places such as concerts, shopping malls, and graveyards. You have stripped a layer from your spirit and are fresh as a newborn baby—and therefore just as vulnerable as one. The blessed oil helps protect you during this time.

Standard Blessing Bath

In the first bath, we removed everything bad from your spirit—but that space needs to be filled with something else until your spirit is fully rejuvenated. It's much like having a large abscess removed; it creates a pocket that the doctors have to fill to prevent further infection or issues. This is a general blessing bath to bring you good health and happiness.

You will need:

- 1 handful dandelion root (better if harvested while the moon is in the chest or Leo)
- 1 handful five-finger grass/cinquefoil
- 3 tablespoons church dirt

Bring a gallon of water to a boil, then add the dandelion root, five-finger grass, and church dirt and return to a boil for 7 minutes. Strain the herbs and let the water cool. Store the infused water in a gallon jug and use a third of the jug per tub of water for each washing, repeating the bath for three days in a row.

Take your normal bath before you take this spiritual bath.

When washing, do so either before the sun rises or as the hand of the clock goes up. Likewise, wash upward from your feet to your head, from your hands to your shoulders. After this bath, either air dry or pat dry with a towel but *do not rub*—otherwise you will be rubbing the work off. After the bath, lightly dust yourself with baby powder.

Again, save a bit of your bathwater to scrub your front doorstep or porch. This sets it further to draw your blessings.

HEAD AND FOOT WASHING

The head and feet are the roof and foundation for the home of the soul. Because of this, they are also the most vulnerable to being the targets for "shots" or "poison"—that is, works placed against you.

Head washings are generally done in living water such as a creek or river, though in the winter they are done indoors. Head washing can be done alone, but it's commonly done with two people, who wash each other while reciting prayers specific to the other person's troubles or issues.

Foot washing is something you may recognize because it is still done in churches all over the South to commemorate the washing Jesus performed on Maundy Thursday before his crucifixion. This is used for cleansing in the same way as the bath, but can in some instances be more powerful when paired with prayers of driving out illnesses and spirits of misfortune. Both can be done simply with pure water and prayer, but they may also include brewed washes, like the standard blessing bath.

Head Washing

To perform a head washing by yourself, go to a creek or fill the kitchen sink with water. (Scrub your sink beforehand so the water is as pure as it can be.) Once it is full of warm water pray Psalm 23 over it seven times (see page 66), then cup some water in your hands and run it over your head. Moisten every part of your head and every strand of hair while praying for your situation. Wrap your head in a white towel or cloth to dry it. If you perform this at night, sleep with the covering over your head. After your hair has dried, dust a bit of baby powder in it for spiritual protection. Head washing is best repeated on the same day every week for three to nine weeks. Avoid crowds for twenty-four hours after each head washing.

Foot Washing

Take up a basin of warm water into which you have stirred 1 table-spoon of new salt bought specifically for foot washing. (Nana used a foot pan and washcloth for washing her feet before going anywhere—even to church, because churches are filled with "sick folk," like a spiritual hospital, and their most cared for aren't always put together and are not always best to be around spiritually.) Pray Psalm 31:1–8 over it while you wash your feet with the washcloth:

> 1 *In thee, O Lord, do I put my trust; let me never be ashamed: deliver me in thy righteousness.*
>
> 2 *Bow down thine ear to me; deliver me speedily: be thou my strong rock, for an house of defence to save me.*
>
> 3 *For thou art my rock and my fortress; therefore for thy name's sake lead me, and guide me.*
>
> 4 *Pull me out of the net that they have laid privily for me: for thou art my strength.*
>
> 5 *Into thine hand I commit my spirit: thou hast redeemed me, O Lord God of truth.*
>
> 6 *I have hated them that regard lying vanities: but I trust in the Lord.*
>
> 7 *I will be glad and rejoice in thy mercy: for thou hast considered my trouble; thou hast known my soul in adversities;*
>
> 8 *And hast not shut me up into the hand of the enemy: thou hast set my feet in a large room.*

It's better to use a white or light-colored washcloth. I have one that I only use for personal foot washing and one for washing others' feet. Clean the cloth afterward by sticking it in a mug or glass and pouring equal parts apple cider vinegar and soda water (water into which baking soda has been dissolved) over the top. Let it sit overnight, then rinse it out and hang it to dry. You can cast out the washing water to the west point of your home.

SWEEPING AND WASHING

Your home is where you spend a large majority of your vulnerable time, especially when sleeping, so it's best to keep it clean physically and spiritually. Clutter in the home can make for "bad air" because it makes it hard for air to circulate and it's believed this can also make you sick. Clutter can also cause depression—another thing that makes you susceptible to spiritual attachments. To keep your home clean and open, sweeping and washing should be performed regularly.

Sweeping

Whenever my mother cleaned the house, in the morning, after the sun rose, she sprinkled Comet for odors and germs in the carpet, and a mixture of baby powder and salt for the "spiritual germs." After sunset, she would either sweep or vacuum it up. She would begin sprinkling from the back of the house and work her way to the front, tossing a bit before her each time she passed through a doorframe to enter another room, to "pierce the Devil's eyes." She did this mostly around the first of every month, but it can be done every few months. When doing this in cleansing, you are cornering the spirit or work until it has no place to go but outside. Powders and salts can also be used for attracting things to the home when laid in the opposite way, sprinkled from the front to the back of the house.

Here are a few recipes for sprinkling salts and powders:

GENERAL CLEANSING SWEEP

- 2 tablespoons salt per room (½ tablespoon per room for hard floors)
- 3 tablespoons lemon rind or 1 tablespoon lemon salt
- 1 tablespoon borax for entire house. (Follow safety instructions on the back of the box. Mama always used 20 Mule Team Borax because it's as strong as twenty mules in cleansing.)

Mix the salt, lemon rind or lemon salt, and borax in a bowl and pray Psalm 23 (see page 66) over it nine times. Sprinkle the mixture around your home as you pray for every negative spirit, entity, or device of the enemy to "flee from the doorframes, from the tiles and cabinets; from every nail and screw and bolt; from every room and shingle and thread of cloth." (Did I mention we're very specific?) Sprinkle from the back of the home to the front door. If you have many floors, work from the back of the topmost floor to the front door on the lower level. After twenty-four hours, sweep up the mixture in the same way.

SWEEP TO REMOVE WITCHCRAFT

- 1 tablespoon borax
- 2 tablespoons salt per room (½ tablespoon per room for hard floors)
- 1 tablespoon asafoetida

Mix the borax, salt, and asafoetida in a bowl. Sprinkle the powder from the back of the house to the front while reciting Psalm 91 three, five, or nine times, depending on how big your home is.

1 He that dwelleth in the secret place of the most High shall abide under the shadow of the Almighty.

2 I will say of the Lord, He is my refuge and my fortress: my God; in him will I trust.

3 Surely he shall deliver thee from the snare of the fowler, and from the noisome pestilence.

4 He shall cover thee with his feathers, and under his wings shalt thou trust: his truth shall be thy shield and buckler.

5 Thou shalt not be afraid for the terror by night; nor for the arrow that flieth by day;

6 Nor for the pestilence that walketh in darkness; nor for the destruction that wasteth at noonday.

7 A thousand shall fall at thy side, and ten thousand at thy right hand; but it shall not come nigh thee.

8 Only with thine eyes shalt thou behold and see the reward of the wicked.

9 Because thou hast made the Lord, which is my refuge, even the most High, thy habitation;

10 There shall no evil befall thee, neither shall any plague come nigh thy dwelling.

11 For he shall give his angels charge over thee, to keep thee in all thy ways.

12 They shall bear thee up in their hands, lest thou dash thy foot against a stone.

13 Thou shalt tread upon the lion and adder: the young lion and the dragon shalt thou trample under feet.

14 Because he hath set his love upon me, therefore will I deliver him: I will set him on high, because he hath known my name.

15 He shall call upon me, and I will answer him: I will be with him in trouble; I will deliver him, and honour him.

16 With long life will I satisfy him, and shew him my salvation.

SWEEP TO REMOVE HAINTS

* 2 tablespoons salt per room (½ tablespoon per room for hard floors)
* 1 tablespoon asafoetida
* 3 shakes of baby powder

Mix the salt and asafoetida and sprinkle enough baby powder over to completely cover it. Stir while reciting Psalm 31:15–17 three times:

15 My times are in thy hand: deliver me from the hand of mine enemies, and from them that persecute me.

16 Make thy face to shine upon thy servant: save me for thy mercies' sake.

17 Let me not be ashamed, O Lord; for I have called upon thee: let the wicked be ashamed, and let them be silent in the grave.

While sprinkling repeat it again three times, telling the spirit to depart in the three highest names. Then take a horseshoe and wrap it in red cloth. Pass through the home after sprinkling, from back to front, with the horseshoe in one hand with points down while telling the spirit to depart and praying the psalm another three times for a total of nine times. Begin by saying "Our Father" and then reciting Psalm 31:15–17.

Washing

Much as the body is the home of the soul and the head and feet are washed, so too is the home spiritually cleaned and washed. This often occurred by prayer and using household products containing botanicals such as pine, orange, mint, or lemon. To these washes salt, baking soda, borax, church dirt, and other things may be added to the bucket with the diluted product. Spiritual washing is done when you feel it's needed or every two to three months. Washing is done for cleansing, protection, or drawing luck, love, or money to the home by washing the doors, windows, counters, cabinets, walls, and floors.

GENERAL CLEANSING WASH

- 1 oz citrus-type soap
- 2 oz Pine-Sol
- 3 tablespoons salt
- 1 capful ammonia
- Splash of white distilled vinegar

Make up a bucket of warm soapy water with Pine-Sol. Then add the salt, ammonia, and vinegar and stir while praying or singing a hymn such as "Great High Mountain" or "His Eye Is on the Sparrow." If you're worried about the wash adversely affecting painted walls or floors, replace the ammonia with 1 capful castor oil.

Wash the walls, doors, and windows from top to bottom. (I recommend sweeping the floors and wiping the walls and windows with a cleaning product first—otherwise you'll just be wiping dust around.) For the floors, begin at the back of the home and move to the front.

After washing, we used sandalwood and cherry incense for blessing the home. Then, following the example of Mamaw Seagle, we would burn asafoetida on the stove. Mama always burned some Indian House Blessing incense too. When lighting the incense, we pray either the Thanksgiving Psalm (150):

> *1 Praise ye the Lord. Praise God in his sanctuary: praise him in the firmament of his power.*
>
> *2 Praise him for his mighty acts: praise him according to his excellent greatness.*
>
> *3 Praise him with the sound of the trumpet: praise him with the psaltery and harp.*
>
> *4 Praise him with the timbrel and dance: praise him with stringed instruments and organs.*
>
> *5 Praise him upon the loud cymbals: praise him upon the high sounding cymbals.*
>
> *6 Let every thing that hath breath praise the Lord. Praise ye the Lord.*

or Psalm 141:1–2:

> *1 Lord, I cry unto thee: make haste unto me; give ear unto my voice, when I cry unto thee.*
>
> *2 Let my prayer be set forth before thee as incense; and the lifting up of my hands as the evening sacrifice.*

SWEEPING THE BODY

The body and spirit are just like the home: it gets cluttered from time to time with general negativity, and "bad wind" can get caught in the spirit from arguing and family feuds, stress, worrisome thoughts, witchcraft, and so on. Sweeping the body agitates these, much like brushing your teeth agitates the bacteria in your mouth. When done on a regular basis, it changes the environment and makes it inhospitable for these spiritual germs. Sweeping can also act in not only a purgative manner, but a protective one as well by removing haint attachments, tricks, and crossings. It chases them away.

Sweeping the body for cleansing should be done weekly. Sweeping doesn't have the same precautions as a cleansing bath, because you're essentially dusting your spirit, and if done regularly, a simple dusting will help in most cases.

Egg Sweeping

One of the first examples of sweeping I ever heard of or saw was done with an egg by Papaw Trivett. He would use an egg to take out illness and even a fever; with the latter, the egg was sometimes hard-boiled by the time he finished.

Through a large influx of Latinx populations into Appalachia between 1950 and 1990, there has been an interchange in recipes and remedies for health and wellness, both physically and spiritually. This likely also contributed to the strong beliefs behind the use of common Catholic saints here, such as Our Lady of Guadalupe and Saint Jude, both patrons of the poor and those in dire situations.

In Mexico, an egg cleansing is one of many methods known altogether as a *limpia*, which literally means "cleaning" or "cleansing." The egg acts like a vacuum, sucking up everything bad from the body and spirit such as disease, heartbreak, grief, fear, curses, and so on. I never learned where Papaw had learned of using the egg, but he did own his own contracting company and employed a lot of Mexican folks, so I suspect he may have heard of it from one of them. Aside from this, there are plenty of records showing that eggs have been used in magico-medical means for healing a variety of things, whether it was taking an egg laid on Good Friday and rubbing it on a boil for a cure, placing the white of an egg on sore eyes, or laying an egg on the chest or beneath the Adam's apple to prevent vomiting. These remedies hold a spiritual element still, one that is uniquely Appalachian, at least going back a few generations.

EGG CLEANSING

You will need:

- White taper candle
- 3 eggs at room temperature (preferably local and/or organic)
- "Holy" water (creek or spring) over which Psalm 23 has been prayed three times daily for seven days (see page 66)
- A clear glass of spring water (not tap water)

Egg cleansings are generally performed on other people, but they may be done solo as well. If you are performing the cleansing on someone else, have the person lay down on the floor, or on a bed or couch. Light your candle while praying Psalm 86:

> *1 Bow down thine ear, O Lord, hear me: for I am poor and needy.*
>
> *2 Preserve my soul; for I am holy: O thou my God, save thy servant that trusteth in thee.*
>
> *3 Be merciful unto me, O Lord: for I cry unto thee daily.*
>
> *4 Rejoice the soul of thy servant: for unto thee, O Lord, do I lift up my soul.*
>
> *5 For thou, Lord, art good, and ready to forgive; and plenteous in mercy unto all them that call upon thee.*
>
> *6 Give ear, O Lord, unto my prayer; and attend to the voice of my supplications.*

7 In the day of my trouble I will call upon thee: for thou wilt answer me.

8 Among the gods there is none like unto thee, O Lord; neither are there any works like unto thy works.

9 All nations whom thou hast made shall come and worship before thee, O Lord; and shall glorify thy name.

10 For thou art great, and doest wondrous things: thou art God alone.

11 Teach me thy way, O Lord; I will walk in thy truth: unite my heart to fear thy name.

12 I will praise thee, O Lord my God, with all my heart: and I will glorify thy name for evermore.

13 For great is thy mercy toward me: and thou hast delivered my soul from the lowest hell.

14 O God, the proud are risen against me, and the assemblies of violent men have sought after my soul; and have not set thee before them.

15 But thou, O Lord, art a God full of compassion, and gracious, long suffering, and plenteous in mercy and truth.

16 O turn unto me, and have mercy upon me; give thy strength unto thy servant, and save the son of thine handmaid.

17 Shew me a token for good; that they which hate me may see it, and be ashamed: because thou, Lord, hast holpen me, and comforted me.

Wash the egg in the holy water and let it cool to room temperature. Once the egg is ready, hold it in your dominant hand about 6 inches above the person. Begin by passing the egg in a cross pattern over the head, chest, and feet. To make the cross, start at the top position of the envisioned cross and go down, then go up, to the right, then to the left. This is blessing and preparing the person for the cleansing. While making each cross, I often pray:

> *Three crosses I make and I beg they do help us, two for*
> *the thieves and one for Christ Jesus.*

Once the crosses are made, pass the egg slowly from head to toe three or seven times while praying the Lord's Prayer (see page 86). This is done for the front, sides, and back of the person, passing three times over each. If you're doing this on yourself, try to cover as much area as you can with passing. Always go from head to toe, never back and forth. Some folks like to pass the egg in counterclockwise circles while going from head to toe.

Once done, crack the egg into the glass of spring water and place the eggshell on a plate. Make the sign of the cross over the glass in the name of the Father, the Son, and the Holy Spirit, and let the yolk sit for about thirty minutes. The resulting formations will show if more cleansing is needed and what or who was the cause.

During the passing, the egg may get really heavy or even break once it's "full," even if you're holding it as gently as you can. In this case, a new egg should be gotten and the procedure continued with the second egg. If that occurs, open the egg in the glass of water and place the shell on the plate. Once done with the second egg, crack it open into the glass and place its shell with the other one.

Egg cleansings are usually done three times in a row with an hour passing between the first and second sessions and thirty minutes between the second and third sessions. Although three passings aren't always needed, depending on what the first egg shows, you should still have the other two eggs handy just in case.

Once the thirty minutes has passed, take note of the formations in the glass.

- If the egg smells bad or has a strong odor, this is a sign of evil being done or severe illness. This is also indicated if the egg shows blood.

- Small spots of blood in the water show signs of bad luck and damage done by witchcraft or conjure, especially if the water is also cloudy or murky.

- If the water becomes cloudy without scent or blood, there's been a loss of vital spiritual energy that needs to be healed. In many folk traditions this is a sign of nightmares, PTSD, depression, or addiction.

- If the egg yolk makes the shape of a face, this is a sign of an enemy. A slender face represents a man; a round face represents a woman.

- If the yolk looks like an eye of sorts, this shows that the evil eye is present and will most likely warrant additional sessions to be removed, paired with other cleansings.

- Small bubbles in the water or egg show that negativity has been removed.

- If the water is clear without any abnormal shapes or scents, then nothing unnatural has occurred and no more cleansings are needed.

- Spider web formations in the white of the egg show that something is blocking or stopping you. Additional sessions are needed to remove any existing problems.

- With egg cleansings, it is expected for the whole egg to sink to the bottom. This shows that all negativity was removed. If any part of the egg floats, another session is needed.

Once you've read the egg and performed any other needed sessions, dispose of the eggs and their shells in a ditch, crossroads, or dumpster. Wash your hands with cheap whiskey afterward. Limit your sessions to three a day. If the third egg shows more work is needed, wait until after the sun rises again to continue.

Aside from the egg, other objects have been used in the same manner for spiritual cleansing as well. Herbs such as goldenrod, tobacco, basil, onion grass, and cedar are swept over the body like a broom from head to toe and then burned to rid disease and witchcraft. You can also use a taper candle. Carve your name in it from wick to bottom and then sweep your body with it from head to toe three times while praying the Lord's Prayer (see page 86). Light it as the sun goes down and let it burn completely in one lighting. Dispose of the candle at a crossroads by burying it in newspaper.

CLEANSING ITEMS

Items need cleansing just as much as people do—especially items that belonged to a deceased person (whom you don't wish haunting you), items from antique stores, statues, and items whose history is unknown. Spirits can hop rides on items and statues or dolls just the same as they can ride a person from one place to another. This especially applies if the item is something tethering a spirit here: they must go wherever the item goes.

When an item needs to be cleansed, there are a few methods I grew up with. One was to take the item to the creek and wash it in the cascades, where the water rushes over stones, making a white reflection. The creek is strongest here and so is its cleansing power. No haint or bad spirit can stay tethered to an item washed in those currents. While washing the item, we sing or pray verses such as Psalm 31:1–5 (see page 89).

Mind you, this is for stuff that water won't ruin. If your item may be ruined by water, then you'll need to get a cedar box. Oil the inside of the box with olive oil that has been blessed by praying Psalm 23 (see page 66) over it. Layer the bottom of the box with salt, baking soda, and pine needles and wait for the sun to rise on a Sunday. As the sun rises, position the opened box so that the rays of the rising sun shine into the box. It was at this point that a hymn is prayed, usually "Blessed Assurance." Placed the item inside the box and keep it closed until the following Sunday, when it is opened to let in the rising sun again. Then the item is cleansed, as nothing can survive that long in that mixture while also pinned up in a cedar box. Anything bad has suffocated, so to speak.

For things that can't be trekked down to the creek or stuffed in a box, you can make up a solution of 1 cup warm water, 1 capful apple cider vinegar, and 1 tablespoon baking soda or saltpeter; then take a wash rag and wipe the item down. Mama and Nana both did this while spring cleaning and dusting, singing hymns such as "Four Days Late," "Blessed Assurance," and "Down in the River to Pray."

After you have spiritually cleaned your body, your home, and any questionable objects, it's time for the next step: protection. Because what's the point in cleaning if you're not going to try to prevent it from getting dirty again? The following practices act as both protection and security systems, keeping you safe and further alerting you of any "breaches" that may occur.

6

SALT UNDER THE ROCKS

ustaining one's own health, spiritually and physically, is vitally important for the majority of Appalachia. The slightest show of disease or bad fortune can decimate a person's entire livelihood, especially if that someone is a main caretaker of the family. This protection also extended to the property and other needed residents such as cattle, pigs, chickens, ducks, and horses, an area that moves into the work of the little-known horse and cow doctors.

Life in Appalachia is a paradox. There is life and death constantly dancing in and out the door in the forms of sickness and health, prosperity and poverty, peace and feuds, angels and demons. Appalachian Americans know firsthand how fragile the fabric of our lives is. One clean swipe from an enemy can knock us completely off the game board. It is here again that faith and superstition take center stage. Both warn us against particular actions and taboos in order to avoid bad luck, illness, or strife. Here I will detail the methods to prevent such things. Of course, none of this work is guaranteed. But with the faith of a mustard seed, you can move mountains. Plus, a little precaution never hurt.

PROTECT AGAINST HAINTS

Haints are a pest to deal with, and if left to their devices, it gets harder and harder to get rid of them. This is why, back in the day, family members were all buried on the property. This way if a haint came to the house, it was far more likely it was a relative and the folks wouldn't be scared and they'd know how to handle it. Nowadays, with folks being buried all over, we have to go through an interview of sorts to test the spirits. But one thing is for certain: if a haint or spirit can get past all of the things we'll cover in this chapter, then they probably don't have bad intentions for you.

Haints include any pesky or malicious spirits, be it an ancestor who lived and died wrong, a wayward spirit that hopped along for the ride, a demon, or some other land entity. These are always spirits that haven't moved on for one reason or another. Some signs of haint activity include items disappearing, moving by themselves, or being tossed and broken on a recurring basis; foul smells, such as rotten eggs; an uneasy, almost nauseating feeling while being in the home, which most of the time disappears as soon as you're off the property; insomnia or nightmares; repeatedly waking up in the middle of the night; hearing sounds such as talking or something falling throughout the house with no known cause. The list goes on, but those are the common signs. If a family member comes to haunt the home, they can enter regardless of anything set up if they lived there in life or have previously been invited in.

A word of caution here: There is one thing in these hills that is worse than a haint, no matter how old, displeased, or forgotten they may be. This is a spirit called a plat-eye, which is the result of a person not being properly buried. Another tale is that plat-eyes are slaves left to die. A slave master would sometimes bury their gold or something real special beneath a tree. Then he'd take his strongest slave and chain him to that tree to guard it, in life and in death. They were left to die there. Not only have they not moved on, but they haven't had a proper burial. The signs of these wronged souls is the sound of chains smacking against a tree; with others, it's a sign of their death—the sound of flowing water if they drowned, air thinning if they suffocated, etc. This happens in a number of situations, whether it's murder victims, folks lost in the hills or swept away by the rivers, or those who went to war and had no family to look for them. It may not seem that common, but here? Anything is possible, and that is sad and true. We've had countless wars. The hills are perfect hiding places. And many people have died in these rivers or have simply gone missing while traveling through the mountains.

Unlike haints, plat-eyes are tethered to this plane, and are connected to more things than just their body. They can change their shape to animals such as black dogs with their guts dragging on the ground or headless roosters, to inanimate objects such as rags hanging from trees, a cloud of fog that hovers with a mind of its own, or some black shapeless thing with piercing yellow or red eyes. One story recounts a plat-eye showing itself as a black cat with glowing eyes, two front legs, and four back legs!

They always have those glowing eyes. Red with anger and rage. They can cause nightmares, insomnia, and more from the boundaries of the property. So if you don't feel like you're being watched inside, but you do feel this way outside, there may be a plat-eye out there. The same protections apply to plat-eyes as haints, but plat-eyes do have a tendency to break salt lines, cast dust on oiled doors (which absorbs the oil and eventually falls off), and more, so be careful. You can carry a bag of gunpowder and sulfur with you or hang one up: they hate this mixture and won't go anywhere near it.

To keep haints and plat-eyes out of the home, hang an old iron, used horseshoe over the door, drive nine used horseshoe nails into the base of the doorframe, mark three crosses over every door with white chalk, or hang garlic, peppers, or onions in the home. Always keep a line of salt at the doors and windows, moistened with whiskey or water to harden it. We also keep a Bible by the door opened to Psalm 23 and a glass of equal parts water and blue dish soap or laundry bluing set out. Mamaw Hopson would hang dried corncobs or windchimes outside the home, on the front porch, in the windows, and in the barn, where the pigs and chickens were kept.

To protect yourself from haints when away from the home, carry the left hind foot of a rabbit with you, sew a piece of red ribbon to the inner heel of each shoe, wear red and black pepper in your shoes, wear a head covering, or wear your socks inside out. Regular cleansing paired with these will also keep haints away from you. I've also known folks to keep a small copy of the Bible on their keys, or a small copy of the Psalms in the glove box of their car. You may also create a charm from Psalm 31:15–17 (see page 204).

Take out all of the vowels, place a period between the words, and replace the Lord's name with three crosses. Begin and end with a cross on each line. Write your name above it with your signature, and carry it with you everywhere:

> +*My.tms.r.n.th.hnd.dlvr.m.frm.th.hnd.f.mn.nms.nd. frm.thm.tht.prsct.m.*+
>
> +*Mk.thy.fc.t.shn.pn.thy.srvnt.sv.m.fr.th.mrcs.sk.*+
>
> +*Lt.m.nt.b.shmd.* +++ *fr.hv.cll.pn.th.lt.th. wckd.b.shmd.nd.lt.thm.b.slnt.n.th.grv.* +

WARD OFF DISEASE

Medical care in Appalachia hasn't been all that great, especially for poor folks who couldn't afford it from the start. Because of this, even with the advent of pills and other pharmaceutical medicines, the majority of folks refused to give up their herbs and roots. Many still drink spring tonics such as sassafras root tea to clean the blood. Likewise, methods were devised and old wives' tales followed to avoid getting ill during the season or coming year by warding off diseases, thought by some to be caused by spirits.

It's said if you catch the first leaf you see falling in autumn, you won't be sick all winter. Turn your pockets inside out at the hooting of an owl to prevent sickness. Another method of warding off illness reaches back to the Cherokee and probably further. They would hang the carcass of a vulture over the door based on the belief that the vulture was immune to every disease and could therefore protect them too. Today, we keep a small bundle of vulture feathers posted over the door. In a pinch, raven or crow feathers will work, but vulture feathers are best. A buzzard's dried head hung about the neck also warded off head colds and headaches.

If one is already sick, you may prevent it from worsening by doing the following: refrain from sweeping that room, especially under the bed, until they are well; don't change the bed sheets unless absolutely necessary, and don't cut their nails until they are well again. Otherwise, it's said it will take their strength away. You can also take a new bottle filled a third of the way with saltwater and hang it up by the head of the bed, to the left, and keep it closed tight to keep haints and witchcraft away. You may also powder the sheets with baby powder and place a Bible beneath the bed opened to John 11:1–45, which details the resurrection of Lazarus. Just as Lazarus was freed from the bonds of death, so will the person be freed from sickness.

AVERT BAD LUCK

Appalachian Americans have always tried their best to avoid the bad cards in the deck life deals by following superstitions and taboos. Averting bad luck was practiced by everyone of all ages, from the old farmer who made sure to plant every row of crops to the school child who would kiss their textbooks after they dropped them. Here's how we avoid bad luck: Never open an umbrella inside, or turn a chair on its leg in the house. Always light a new candle and put it out. Never exit a door you didn't enter from. Always step into your home with your right foot first. Turn your pockets inside out upon a black cat or a white "witch" rabbit crossing your path from the right to the left. If you spill salt, toss some over your left shoulder to blind the Devil. Never whistle outside at night. If you drop a comb, put your foot on it first before picking it up. Never comb your hair in the dark, as the saying goes: "Comb your hair in the dark, comb your sorrows to your heart; comb your hair in the day, comb your sorrows away." It is also bad luck to shave in March. And marry. And move. March is just a bad month in general.

You can also wear new salt in your shoes to bring success in all your undertakings, or wear a penny issued in your birth year. But it has to be the first one for that date that you find in the year. Pennies and dimes issued during leap years also bring good luck. Specific luck in love, money, and business will be discussed further.

PROTECT AGAINST WITCHCRAFT

As we've seen, even the kindest of neighbors may have something against you. Today, they may not curse your cows or horses, but witchcraft can still bring about strange illnesses for which there is no cure, horrible fortune in money and employment, and strife to a whole household. While the belief in witches and witchcraft has diminished greatly, and with its passing the witchdoctors as well, the power it has is still there, unbeknownst to those who come victim to it. This social belief transition first began in the valleys in the cities, where the more "sophisticated" folks lived. They prided themselves on their "civilized" manners and beliefs, unlike those hicks who still lived in the mountains and woods. That's not to say that city dwellers had no superstitions or taboos; they simply weren't as numerous and didn't hold the same sway on life as they did for the mountain dweller. This can be seen in the different types of omens held by both groups.

In the mountain regions of Virginia, Tennessee, North Carolina, and Georgia, in the late nineteenth and early twentieth centuries, stories spread of a "belled buzzard" who flew close to the ground with a bell around its neck that went *ding . . . ding . . . ding*, the prior ring toning out before the next rang. Wherever it landed, it predicted death for the owner of the land or home. The belled buzzard, whether real or phantom apparition, was last seen on Friday, August 13, 1926. It could have only been one buzzard, but they generally live twenty years, and the belled buzzard reports spanned sixty-plus years.

While death was predicted by a musically inclined bird in the mountains, death was foretold by the arrival of a white horse, a recalling symbol of the horseman in Revelations. In the valleys, a pregnant woman shouldn't look at a white horse or it would cause trouble in labor. To dream of a white horse predicted death, and the birth of a white mare on the farm was bad luck. However, in the mountains the white horse was considered an otherworldly being, with its hair and shoes having strong powers against witchcraft. It is also included in folk remedies, such as one to cure colic that calls for drinking water after a white horse.

So while superstitions have changed greatly in the southern hill countries of Tennessee, Virginia, North Carolina, and Kentucky, the needs and wants of the people remain the same. To protect against witchcraft, hang a horseshoe wrapped in tinfoil ("silver paper," as it was called) over the front door, or hang a pair of opened scissors, points down, over the windows. Never let a stranger or neighbor you've had it out with borrow anything. When having company over, hide all combs and brushes, lest your company snag some hair during their visit. Take a tablespoon of castor oil on the first of every month, or drink sassafras tea to strengthen the body and spirit against roots placed against you.

Wear a silver dime, minted in 1964 or prior, around the neck or ankles. Many roots and powders used for cursing contain sulfur, which reacts to the dime and turns it black in the process of taking the hit for you and also warns you that you've "walked over poison."

PROTECT LIVESTOCK

To protect livestock from conjuring, take four brown paper bags and fill them with equal parts asafoetida, whole red peppers, salt, snuff dipped in vinegar, and a cross (this can be hand made from two sticks). Hand these around the livestock area. You may also hang up a horseshoe, points down, wrapped in one full newspaper. Catch the first rainwater in May and sprinkle it on the animals once a month or give it to them in their drink. Take candles dipped on Christmas night and burn them, dripping the wax around the premises. To protect animals from the evil eye, sprinkle them with blessed water or holy water from a Catholic church.

GENERAL PROTECTION FOR LOVED ONES NEAR AND FAR

A general protection my grandparents always used was to take a person's photo or name and place it in the folds of a Bible at Psalm 23 or another protective verse facedown toward the verse.

For soldiers, place it at Ephesians 6:11:

> Put on the whole armour of God, that ye may be able to
> stand against the wiles of the devil.

For little children, especially if they are in potentially unsafe environments, place it at Matthew 18:10:

> Take heed that ye despise not one of these little ones; for
> I say unto you, That in heaven their angels do always
> behold the face of my Father which is in heaven.

This can also be done with a small item of the person's. After my nephew was born, we did this with his little booties and placed them in one of Nana's old Bibles. Lastly, if a loved one has been gone for a while and you wish to call them home, turn a photo of them on its head until they return.

PROTECT AGAINST WEAPONS AND ASSAULT

For most of its colonized life, the hills of Appalachia have been filled with violence and crime, from bootlegging deals gone wrong to deadly family feuds. This has always been a threat, especially if you find yourself in the company of the wrong people. When the Civil War and the World Wars came, pocket Bibles were marketed to the public with the allegations that, if carried over the heart on the battlefield, they would stop a bullet and save your life. Other charms, conjure bags, and written verses were carried by the faithful and still are to this day. Here are a few verses and written charms that may be carried with you:

Ephesians 6:11 written as follows:

> *[Your Name]*
>
> *+Put on*
>
> *the whole armour of*
>
> *+++, [Your Name] that ye may be able to*
>
> *stand against the wiles of the devil +++*

Carry a written SATOR square. Used in European folk magic, a few charms have been found in old shoes, plastered into walls, and more from Tennessee to Ohio, Pennsylvania, and West Virginia. The square's true meaning is unknown, as is its true origin. Following are a couple of variations.

O+++*X*X*X*+++O

SATOR

AREPO

TESET

ROTAS

O + I I I + O

Finally, you may also use the Paternoster cross (opposite page), which is Latin for "Our Father." I have not found any sources in southern Appalachia for its use but it has been used in northern Appalachia. The *A* and *O* symbolize alpha and omega. Draw it in chalk on the walls.

Lastly, another form is the same as the SATOR square, but also contains the powerful abbreviations of INRI and CMB, that is the inscription on the cross at Calvary and the first initials of each of the three wise men:

+ I N + R I +

SATOR

AREPO

TENET

OPERA

ROTAS

C. + M. + B. +

```
A                    P                    O
                     A
                     T
                     E
                     R
         P A T E R   N O S T E R
                     O
                     S
                     T
                     E
O                    R                    A
```

CONJURE BAG FOR PROTECTION

Most conjurers and even plain folks carried a personal conjure bag made by themselves or acquired from a conjure doctor to protect them from all evil and danger, whether accidents, criminals, rabid animals, snakebites, haints, or witchcraft. Again, items that have a protective quality in the mind of the mountain folks have been used for such things, much like pretty, flowering herbs and heart-shaped leaves are used in love conjuring. These items range from common things such as garlic, onion skins, dried minnows, and hair to the more obscure "wood from where two trees rub together in the wind," or "skin from a church snake." The following is an example of awakening a poke or hex bag in general and a recipe for protection from the above threats. The best bags are those blessed over a long period of time. With protection bags for personal use, bless them three times in total: once when the moon is in the head (Aries), once when it is in the heart (Leo), and once when it is in the feet (Pisces). Always keep your ingredients at an odd number so "it can't be cut in half" by your enemies. Whiskey, personal concerns such as your hair or name, and baby powder aren't ingredients, but more fuel and eyes, feeding the bag and letting it see for you in order for it to do its job.

Everyone makes their hex and conjure bags differently, and I use different methods based on the work at hand and how the Spirit is leading me. The following is one of my methods.

You will need:

- White taper candle
- Tobacco smoke or incense such as frankincense or myrrh
- 4-inch by 4-inch piece of blue flannel
- 4-inch by 4-inch piece of newspaper
- Your hair or nail clippings from every finger and toe
- Red string or yarn
- Snuff soaked in vinegar for three days and strained
- A glass of water that has been blessed by reciting the Lord's Prayer over it three times (see page 86)
- Whiskey
- Baby powder
- New salt
- Asafoetida

Light your candle while reciting Psalm 23 (see page 66), and light your incense while praying Psalm 141:1–2 (see page 95).

Take your piece of flannel and lay it flat. Over the top lay the piece of newspaper, which is used against witchcraft because whatever is being sent to you has to count every letter on it first. Yes, count. Roots contain small spirits or pieces of the witch, and that's what gives them life.

On the newspaper, add the hair and nail clippings, snuff, salt, and asafoetida while praying something along the lines of the following:

> *No water or fire, no weapon of any material may harm me. No accidents or illness can befall me, no ghostly things haunt me, and no witchcraft may claw me, for I have three persons over me. The first is the Father, the second is the Son, and the third is the Holy Ghost. Whoever or whatever is as strong as these may approach me and rip me to pieces. Until then, I am protected by the five wounds and a death shroud does not hug my shoulders.*

Make the sign of the cross over the herbs, from top to bottom, then left to right. Place your hair or nails in the center of the small pile and bring up the corners of the newspaper and flannel to form a small bag. Tie the string around the neck of the poke and secure it with three knots, one for each person of the Trinity.

Now it is time to bring your bag to life. It is customary to name it something only you will know.

> *In the name of the Father, the Son, and the Holy Spirit, wake up, [name]! Rise and do your work for me and only me.*

State your name over the bag three times. Hold it over the candle, far enough away so as not to scorch or burn it, to "cook" the root. Pray that it comes to life, moves when trouble is near, and always protects you from all danger.

Smoke it in the incense or with tobacco smoke:

The same breath that filled Adam's lungs now fills you.
Come to life, [name]. It's time to wake up now.

Sprinkle water over the bag, baptizing it in your name:

By the Father, Son, and Holy Ghost, I baptize you in my
name. Wake up now.

When you have completed this, hold the bag firmly in your left fist and "pump" it to the rhythm of a heartbeat. *Boomboom. Boomboom. Boomboom.*

Do this until your hand gets warm, then breathe three times into your fist against the bag.

It's alive and needs food. Feed it every Sunday by pouring a bit of whiskey on the bag. Then powder it with baby powder. Carry it as close to your skin as you can. Folks usually wear their bag around their neck and under their clothes.

Never let the conjure bag touch the ground or be handled by anyone but you. To do so may make the spirit in it leave. If such a thing occurs, with any kind of conjure bag, take it apart and bury the items in different places.

There are some occasions when your bag may disappear and reappear again in a place you never put it. I've had this happen usually when I forget to feed it. It wanders off on its own to get a drink, basically. Don't do this too many times, though. Not only will the bag die, but it may never come back to you.

If you follow these rules, your bag will last a while; and the longer you carry it, the stronger it gets! There will come a time that it begins to fall apart, at which point you just need to take another piece of flannel and newspaper and wrap it the same as before, tying it off at the neck and feeding it. When this happens, I let the bag rest for three days in a dark box before carrying it with me again.

PROTECTION LAMP

Everybody had kerosene lamps back in the day, so it's no wonder they made their way into this magic. They were often made of metal and glass or clear and colored glass, with the basin being colored, which meant the contents of the basin were hard to see aside from the oil levels. I have an old oil lamp that belonged to Mamaw Seagle, one that she always had going, sitting on my working space now. The old wick is hanging on a hook and has unreadable writing on it in either pen or marker.

While candles took time to be made and, for workings, needed to be burned back to back, the conjure lamp burned for a good month before needing to be refilled. And while candles are rolled in herbs and powders, or "loaded" from the bottom by hollowing out the bottom and putting the herbs in the candle and sealing it back, oil lamps are loaded simply by placing the ingredients in the basin, whether it be hair, roots, or bark wrapped in a small bundle. The petition or prayer is attached to the part of the wick that stays in the basin to fuel the flame or, in the case of Mamaw, it is written on the flat wick. For wicks that are a simple string nowadays, you can roll the paper around the wick and pin it in place by wrapping it with a paper clip. There will be more uses for both candles and lamps later on, but the following is a recipe for a protection lamp to keep burning to protect the home or family against witchcraft.

You will need:

- New oil lamp
- Vinegar
- Baking soda

- Your petition and personal concerns such as hair, nails, a strip of unwashed clothing
- Red pepper
- Black pepper
- Snuff (we use Grizzly or Copenhagen)
- Asafoetida
- Dirt from a ditch
- 5-inch by 5-inch piece of brown paper bag
- Red string

First cleanse your oil lamp by washing it in a solution of 1 cup water, ½ cup vinegar, and 1 tablespoon baking soda while praying Psalm 23 three times (see page 66).

Once it has dried, attach your petition to the wick or write it on it. Place your personal concerns in first or those of the one you wish to protect. These can be one thing from each member of the household as well.

Take the red and black pepper, snuff, asafoetida, and dirt from a ditch and wrap them in a bundle in the brown paper and tie it off with a red string.

Place the bundle inside on top of the concerns and fill the basin with oil. Once it is full, pray Psalm 44:1–7 three times as the hand of the clock goes down from 12 to 6, whether morning or night:

> *1 We have heard with our ears, O God, our fathers have told us, what work thou didst in their days, in the times of old.*
>
> *2 How thou didst drive out the heathen with thy hand, and plantedst them; how thou didst afflict the people, and cast them out.*

3 For they got not the land in possession by their own sword, neither did their own arm save them: but thy right hand, and thine arm, and the light of thy countenance, because thou hadst a favour unto them.

4 Thou art my King, O God: command deliverances for Jacob.

5 Through thee will we push down our enemies: through thy name will we tread them under that rise up against us.

6 For I will not trust in my bow, neither shall my sword save me.

7 But thou hast saved us from our enemies, and hast put them to shame that hated us.

Once you have prayed over the herbs and concerns, blow your breath into the basin three times in the name of the Trinity and close the basin. Then light the flame and let it burn until 6 P.M. Never let the lamp run totally out of oil. Not only will this not be good for the work, but it also brings bad luck.

The body and the home aren't all that need protecting, though. There are threats that can affect your income as well, and the stability of the home itself. Let's turn now to stimulating or tying up money to gain or to cause loss.

1

A DIME, A DOLLAR

Appalachian Americans have made a living in more ways than can be counted, whether it's farming livestock for meat, milk, or eggs; growing tobacco, corn, and other crops; root digging for ginseng, galax, moss, bloodroot, or goldenseal; hunting for hogs, deer, and bears; or mining coal or loading timber, we are resourceful and stubborn. While our ways of live are changing from farming and root hunting to retail and fast food, we still need to keep the lights on and food on the table. The scenes may change, but the needs of the people don't. The following are some recipes for bringing money, paying customers, luck, and employment.

TO FIX YOURSELF FOR MONEY

After taking a cleansing bath, powder your hands and feet with arrowroot powder. (Papaw Trivett used arrowroot powder for luck and success whenever he went down to the casinos, made a business deal, or bought a house to fix up and flip. It was one of the only roots I know of him using, but he had luck with it every time.) Then sprinkle new salt in your shoes or anoint yourself with oil over which Deuteronomy 28:1–8 has been recited seven times:

> *1 And it shall come to pass, if thou shalt hearken diligently unto the voice of the Lord thy God, to observe and*

to do all his commandments which I command thee this day, that the Lord thy God will set thee on high above all nations of the earth:

2 And all these blessings shall come on thee, and overtake thee, if thou shalt hearken unto the voice of the Lord thy God.

3 Blessed shalt thou be in the city, and blessed shalt thou be in the field.

4 Blessed shall be the fruit of thy body, and the fruit of thy ground, and the fruit of thy cattle, the increase of thy kine, and the flocks of thy sheep.

5 Blessed shall be thy basket and thy store.

6 Blessed shalt thou be when thou comest in, and blessed shalt thou be when thou goest out.

7 The Lord shall cause thine enemies that rise up against thee to be smitten before thy face: they shall come out against thee one way, and flee before thee seven ways.

8 The Lord shall command the blessing upon thee in thy storehouses, and in all that thou settest thine hand unto; and he shall bless thee in the land which the Lord thy God giveth thee.

Back in the day, a lot of folks all over the country carried or wore lucky encased pennies. The encasing had lucky symbols fashioned around the coin such as a four-leaf clover, a wish bone, and a horseshoe. They often had such sayings as "Keep Me and Never Go Broke" or "Carry Me and Have Good Luck," which were sometimes shortened to "KMANGO" or "CMAHGL." The one I wear is from Rock City, Lookout Mountain, in Tennessee.

There always comes a time that your luck in money may seem like it is running out. Bills eat everything and you can't hold a dollar tight enough to make the eagle scream. It's possible your luck has changed, but it's also possible you may have been crossed up in some way. To change your luck around and uncross your money, wash your feet in a solution of warm water and your own urine for a week. Sounds awful, but it works mighty fine!

ATTRACT MONEY

Different things have been used for money in Appalachia, from bear, deer, and coon skins to coins and even playing cards. A lot of the "money" used back in the day was simply items traded off for other things of value. Things that were up for offer included pigs, cattle, mules, beans, corn, and bread. Many practitioners, especially the midwives, accepted these in return for their services. I've been given chickens, turkeys, deerskins, bear fat, whiskey, and more in return for my charms and roots. Attracting money is nothing more than sweetening up your luck in business and trade. Here are a few ways to do it:

- Soak a used horseshoe in whiskey for three days as the moon grows. Wash your hands with this whiskey whenever you head to make a business deal.

- Carry the left hind foot of a gray rabbit in your left pocket and feed it with arrowroot powder by powdering it down. Carry it with the toes pointed upward.

- Take two white candles and inscribe your name on one and "Money" on the other. Anoint them with olive oil, rubbing upward from bottom to top while praying Psalm 23:1 seven times: "The Lord is my shepherd; I shall not want."

  - Take an empty tin can and pour some wax from the candle down in the center and fix your name candle on top. Surround the candle with salt, cornmeal, and snuff dipped in molasses.

- Place the money candle in a candle holder to the far left of the first.

- Burn both candles as the sun rises or as the hand of the clock goes up for one hour every day for seven days, each day moving the money candle closer and closer to your candle while continuing your prayers and the recitation of Psalm 23:1.

- Carry a buckeye in your pocket and feed it with whiskey every full moon.

- Take the ten of diamonds from a deck of cards and write your name on it three times horizontally. Then turn it to the right and write your name three times again, crossing over the previous writing to form a sort of tic-tac-toe. Write these with your date of birth between the names each time. Fold the card toward you three times, then bind it to a dried ginseng root with red string that has been anointed with your first urine of the day. Baptize it as you would a poke bag and feed it with a few drops of whiskey.

- Carry powdered Chewing John or Low John with a mixture of baby powder, cinnamon, and arrowroot powder each month. Never let anyone else touch it.

DRAW PAYING CUSTOMERS

Running a business was oftentimes the main income for a family, whether it was selling things at the local farmer's market or flea market, or selling shoes, saddles, and other leather goods. However, times get hard, and paying customers run thin; and there's no point in selling if nobody's buying. This was a type of work especially done by folks who lived in the valley cities such as Knoxville. Whether they learned it themselves or they bought the charm from a conjurer for a pretty penny, they put it to use to help their business.

- Make a solution of warm water, your first morning's urine, sugar, buckeye shavings, and whiskey. Wash your floors and doorstep (or sidewalk) with the solution. Do so in the morning and work your way from the front of the store to the back.

- Place a 4-inch by 7-inch piece of coon skin in a brown paper bag with a scrap of red flannel and some brown beans. Moisten the contents with whiskey while praying Psalm 4:6–7:

   6 There be many that say, Who will shew us any good?
   Lord, lift thou up the light of thy countenance upon us.

   7 Thou hast put gladness in my heart, more than in the
   time that their corn and their wine increased.

- Repeat this on the first Friday of every month.

- Burn red onion skins in the store every Thursday before opening.

- Scrub the doorstep with a brine made from washing rainbow trout in saltwater.

- Fill the bottom of a glass jar with quarters and cornmeal. Cover this with some dirt from the business's property. Fill it with sweet syrup. Close the jar tight and roll it toward you on the floor from the door of the store to you. Roll it a total of twenty-one times every Thursday while praying Psalm 4:6–7 (see page 125). On the other days, shake it at least three times a day while praying for customers to come in and buy from you.

MONEY CONJURE CHARM

To attract money, take one of your left socks, worn but not washed, and write your initials on it going from toe to heel and surround it with money symbols: **$$$ J. M. S. $$$**. Cover this with a dab of molasses. Sprinkle ginger root shavings, dirt from a bank, hair from a white rabbit, tobacco, and arrowroot powder on top. Roll the sock toward you, from toe to heel. Once it is completely rolled up, roll it to you six more times for a total of seven while saying Psalm 23:1: "The Lord is my shepherd; I shall not want." Wrap the bundle in new string, wrapping toward you by curling the string under and over and under and over again. Tie it off with three knots. Carry this with you to attract money and feed it on the first Friday of every month with a bit of whiskey.

CONJURE JAR FOR EMPLOYMENT

Jar workings were a common form of tricking in these hills, and they were able to be hidden just as easily as a conjure lamp. See, back in the day every family had canned goods stored in the basement or in the spring house (a separate building that was usually underground), including canned soups and tomatoes, pickles, okra, or corn. It was quite easy to take a jar filled with conjured roots and hide it among these other jars in the back and on a high shelf. Then every day you'd go down there to "get something" and you'd work the jar while you were down there, whether that consisted of shaking it or rolling it toward you.

Candles weren't burned on jar workings in Appalachia. Jar workings done this way in the Deep South are usually for longer works that take a while. For that, we'd just make up a conjure lamp and keep that burning, its contents being hidden by the colored kerosene or colored glass of the lamp basin. Jars were worked for the same things lamps were, usually after some of the lamps had works in them. It'd be odd to have five or ten lamps burning throughout the home, especially when the homes back then only had one to three rooms, maybe more for folks with a bit more money.

For the jar, you'll need:

- The heel cut from your worn left sock
- Ginseng root
- Syrup
- Low John (trillium)
- Sugar
- Fresh spring water (distilled)
- Molasses

Bless each ingredient as you add it to the jar to have it bring you good luck in gaining work:

> May this ginseng, old mountain climber, help me climb
> that mountain to find good work.
> [Psalm 90:17]
>
> May this syrup sweet every man whose door I knock on
> for work.
> [Psalm 90:17]
>
> May this Low John show the beauty of my work to all
> who see it.
> [Psalm 90:17]
>
> May this sugar sweeten each one whose hand I shake.
> [Psalm 90:17]
>
> May this water bring clarity in the agreements I
> undertake.
> [Psalm 90:17]
>
> May this molasses sweeten each opportunity I meet.
> [Psalm 90:17]

Place your piece of worn sock in the bottom of a glass jar, then fill with a bit of the roots and equal parts water and syrup, the entire time praying Psalm 90:17 after adding each ingredient, for a total of seven times:

> *And let the beauty of the Lord our God be upon us: and establish thou the work of our hands upon us; yea, the work of our hands establish thou it.*

Once the jar is filled and the lid is shut tight, face the east and shake it while praying that you find work soon. Pray from the heart here. Then stay facing your front door or driveway and roll the jar on the ground toward you twenty-one times. After this, set the jar down somewhere high up, taller than you, preferably. Every day, shake the jar and pray and roll it toward you in the same manner until you get the job. Once you've been employed, bury the jar in your front yard.

GOOD HUNTING CONJURE BAG

Hunting game is not only a sport but a necessity for many families in Appalachia today, especially when the monthly check is late and the cabinets are going bare. Deer, hogs, bears, squirrels, possums, and raccoons have all been hunted around here, and good luck charms were sometimes taken to help ensure you got what you needed for the home. My father often carried an airplane bottle of Jägermeister ("buck's blood," as it was sometimes called) with him when he went hunting for deer or turkeys. He said it was because of the cross over the deer's head; it's like your prayers were already answered for a good hunt. I was further convinced when I found out that the emblem for their logo was inspired by the German saint Hubertus, patron of hunting! The Cherokee also carried different charms for success in hunting, so it is a long tradition in the hill country. Here is a hunting conjure bag recipe many of my folks have had success with.

Items needed:

* Tobacco

* Red powdered clay (native to land)

* White mustard seed

* Ginseng root

* If hunting bears, blackberries; deer, apple seeds; turkeys, oats; hogs, lovage or bo' hog root; raccoons, squirrels, or possums, salt

Tie up your tobacco, clay, mustard seed, ginseng, and animal-specific plant in a square of cow leather or red flannel and bless it, calling it up and baptizing it. Recite these verses three times each:

> *He was a mighty hunter before the Lord: wherefore it is said, Even as Nimrod the mighty hunter before the Lord. (Genesis 10:9)*

> *And whatsoever man there be of the children of Israel, or of the strangers that sojourn among you, which hunteth and catcheth any beast or fowl that may be eaten; he shall even pour out the blood thereof, and cover it with dust. (Leviticus 17:3)*

Repeat these verses when you field dress an animal as well; cover the spilled blood with dirt and leaves. (This also connects to a Chero-kee story where the blood of a bear is covered, and as the hunter walks away with the parts and meat, the bear rises again from the earth and goes back into its cave.)

Once you've blessed your bag, feed it with a bit of Jägermeister before sunrise when you head out. Carry it under your left armpit by tying it around your shoulder. When you see game, squeeze it under your arm for luck. When you come home with good game, feed the bag with rendered fat from the animal and place it in a cedar box until your next hunt.

GOOD FISHING HEX BAG

You will need:

- 4-inch by 4-inch piece of newspaper
- White mustard seed
- Walnut leaves
- 3 dried minnow heads
- 4-inch by 4-inch mesh net from a potato sack

Lay out the piece of newspaper and place the mustard seed, walnut leaves, and minnow heads in the center. Recite Ezekiel 47:9–10 nine times over them:

> 9 And it shall come to pass, that every thing that liveth, which moveth, whithersoever the rivers shall come, shall live: and there shall be a very great multitude of fish, because these waters shall come thither: for they shall be healed; and every thing shall live whither the river cometh.

> 10 And it shall come to pass, that the fishers shall stand upon it from Engedi even unto Eneglaim; they shall be a place to spread forth nets; their fish shall be according to their kinds, as the fish of the great sea, exceeding many.

Then tie up the corners into a bag with three knots. Cover that with the mesh net and bind it the same way. When you take it fishing, feed the bag by dipping it in the waters you're fishing from three times in the name of the Trinity, spit on it, and place it to rest on the side of the bucket you plan to put your catch in; you can hang it with a fishing hook on the side. When you've caught what you need, bury the sack on the bank of the river with three angleworms and leave without looking back. Don't count your fish until you get home.

LAMP TO KEEP MONEY FLOWING IN

Much like water, money runs thin or even goes dry. This happens a lot, but it may be prevented by working a conjure lamp for a steady flow of money wherever and however possible. Get a clean oil lamp and fill the basin with a rattlesnake rattle, cornmeal, snuff, seven dimes, and a pinch of dirt from your front door. Wrap this in brown paper and place it in the basin while reciting Psalm 23 (see page 66) twenty-three times, then light the lamp and let it burn as the hand of the clock or the sun rises. Recite Psalm 23 twenty-three times on the first of every month when lighting it.

LUCKY DAYS AND UNLUCKY DAYS

To calculate the lucky days for a month, count the number of days from that full moon to the end of the month. So say the full moon is on January 18. That's thirteen days to the thirty-first. Multiply this by the number of days in the month, so 13 x 31. This equals 403. By this result, the lucky days are the third and the fourth. These days are fortunate for all things, but especially in regards to general luck and money.

To determine the unlucky days in a month, follow the same formula except count the days from the first of the month up to the full moon. So if the full moon is on January 18, your number would be 17.

17 x 31 days in the month is 527. So the unlucky days would be the fifth and the twenty-seventh.

Note: If an unlucky day turns out to be a previously found lucky day, it is marked off and is considered unlucky.

Do this for every month to determine its luck or lack thereof. It's bad to plant, marry, move, lend, and bathe on unlucky days. However, as we'll see soon enough, these days can be correlated with the signs for workings. For love, you could find a lucky day that falls in the sign of the heart (Leo). For cursing, you may find an unlucky day in the sign of the head (Aries).

Now, as the history and plight of Appalachia has shown, money and making a living doesn't always sit on the legal side. As such, many folks have run-ins with the law or try to avoid it in the activities of their illicit professions. Other times, good folks are done plain wrong by the justice system and need a greater power to get them out of the mess they've been thrown in. All of this is undertaken beneath the eyes of the one who dined with thieves and murderers and who will be the Judge to judge all others. The Just Judge.

8

AIN'T NO BADGE THAT
SHINES BRIGHTER

ong before localized authorities, folks often took justice into their
own hands to protect their loved ones and their property, and to
exact revenge. There are hundreds of examples of folks working in and
outside the law here: bootleggers or "wildcats" killing for their jar of
corn, thieves and murderers who've had the Devil whisper in their ear.
Violence and bloodshed have been in the back rows of Appalachian
culture forever. It sits rights next to witchcraft.

In my hometown, Johnson City, Tennessee, it's said there are
underground tunnels leading in and out of the city that were used by
the famous American gangster Al Capone for bootlegging liquor during
Prohibition. Ten minutes west in my current town of Jonesborough,
nearly every house downtown has old tunnels and hideaways used to
traffic and store liquor. Before that, they were used to help slaves in the
Underground Railroad. This type of conjure and folk magic has had
many developments and additions over the centuries. From using "witch
guns" to keep the law off the property to escaping slaves sprinkling graveyard dirt as they went to hide their tracks and throw off the hounds, we
are a people constantly running from our past and our future.

Many folks feared going to the big house, so they'd do everything they could to avoid it. Now before you say, "Well, just don't

do liquor," it wasn't that easy. Moonshine and liquor were big parts of our culture and heritage. They still are. Mind you, we're also stubborn as hell, and most wouldn't quit their stills if the Big Man Upstairs told them himself to stop. Many folks laid powders and bags around the property, and hung rags and other odd but not easily noticed things to either keep the law away or make them sweet. If those didn't work, there were other things to make sure your trial and the judge were in your favor. This is how folks made a living. It paid well and kept food on the table. People still bootleg moonshine; I've had some come to me for a bit of something extra. What folks do isn't my business, so I give them what they ask, whether that's a powder or poke bag.

SWEETEN OFFICERS OF THE LAW

Sometimes the cops get called. Growing up, they were at our house a lot, called by some of Mama's enemies in the neighborhood. But each time they walked in and walked out with a smile, leaving tracks in the salt and cinnamon dust sprinkled on the floor. Officers were also called out to houses that sold liquor secretly, under the guise of a party going on. At these points, powders may be sprinkled to sweeten up law enforcement, and the liquor was hidden. Some folks just get nervous by the law or don't want them around to begin with. To sweeten officers of the law:

- Powder angleworms and lightning-struck wood together with sugar, salt, and cinnamon. Fill a poke bag with the mixture and bury it beneath the doorstep, sprinkling some of the powder in the hole before placing the bag on top. Cover with a layer of dirt, sprinkle more powder, then more dirt and more powder. Finally, cover it completely with dirt and spit on it three times in the name of the Trinity, saying, "Every officer of the law that here should trod shan't take me away till this root by worms be gnawed."

- Sprinkle a mixture of cinnamon, black pepper, and sugar around the room before opening the door. Don't take too long, though, and make sure to sprinkle some at the doorway.

KEEP OFFICERS OF THE LAW AWAY

Maybe you don't care to sweeten anyone up and you'd rather they all just stay gone and far away. These are for that:

- Nail four Indian Head pennies above the doorframe of the front door outside. Papaw wore an Indian Head penny in his bolo tie when he went drinking, in case any trouble started. If bad business takes place in the home, nail nine pennies instead of four.

- Take three fronds of bear's-bed or Christmas fern and lay them parallel to a dried corncob that has been dusted with baby powder, black pepper, and anthill dirt. Tie the fronds around the cob to make a long bundle. Make sure the fronds are tied tight so the cob doesn't fall out. Sprinkle the bundle with olive oil while reciting the Lord's Prayer (see page 86). Place it in a large bucket or crock outside your door that has been filled with ditchwater. Cover this up and stir it on the first of every month while repeating your prayers that the law stays far away from your property and won't cause any trouble.

- Make a hex bag to carry on you or put in your car, which consists of cattail root, cinnamon, Chewing John (galangal root), grapevine bark, and black mustard seeds. While making this bag, say: "Officer John and Samuel Doe, come hither and stub your toe; roll down the hill and in the creek, can't wash off, can't get clean. Don't come back, now nor ever; til my horse gives birth to a red and black heifer." Feed the bad with a powder blessed the same, made up of Chewing John, black pepper, and salt every Friday.

- Take the same powder given above and sprinkle it in the four corners of every room. Dust yourself with it as well as any merchandise.

- Take the footprint of an officer, when you're able to; pick it up from heel to toe. Use the dirt if that's what you're able to get; if it's a moist napkin, let it dry then burn it to ash. Add some of this to a powder like the one above for added potency in keeping all local law enforcement away.

- Take dirt from a police station and mix it with black pepper, black mustard seeds, deer's eye root (black-eyed Susan), and hair from the left hind foot of a white rabbit. Divide mixture into four parts and place each part into its own cloth pouch. Hang each pouch in the four corners of the home.

BRING DOWN THE LAW ON SOMEONE

There have always been those few individuals who seem to get away with everything, or when they get caught, they're simply sent away with nothing but fines and a slap on the wrist. However, Justice always shows up where and especially when she is needed. The following recipes are ones I have personally found effective in putting the law on someone's heels.

- Take some horsehair and river clay. Mold these into a ball, mixing in the person's foot track with it. If this or some other concern is unavailable, use a photo of them. If they have been arrested before, it's more effective to use their mug shot. Once this is made, wrap the ball in white fabric (white to bring everything to the light of day, no secrets) and sew it together. (This is tougher than tied string.) Saturate the ball with water in which you have washed your feet against this person. When you wash, pray against them, naming the bad deeds they have committed against you or others, and pray for the full force of the law to come down upon them. Bury the bag where you know they will walk over it.

- Take some cattail root and angleworm powder. Mix these with flour, black pepper, and guinea pepper. Place this in a glass bottle filled halfway with vinegar and something of theirs. Wrap some black electric tape around the bottle to keep out the light of day. Write down the address of your local jail on a piece of paper and roll the bottle toward it every day as the moon wanes.

- Take some dirt from the police station and jail and mix it with black pepper and snuff. Bury this mixture on the person's property or where they will walk over it.

- Carve the person's name into a candle. Roll the candle away from you and powder it with black pepper. Burn this while praying Isaiah 24:21–22 five times to fix them there. Burn as the hand of the clock goes down.

> 21 And it shall come to pass in that day, that the Lord shall punish the host of the high ones that are on high, and the kings of the earth upon the earth.
>
> 22 And they shall be gathered together, as prisoners are gathered in the pit, and shall be shut up in the prison, and after many days shall they be visited.

HAVE FAVOR IN COURT

There does come a time when you are brought before the judge, either by your own doing or that of someone else. Whether you are in the right or wrong is subjective when it comes to folk magic and conjure. Many a judge and jury have been swayed by the pull of the town's root man for his client, and many have spoken self-convicting truth to the rhythm of his teeth grinding roots. No power has stood a test to that of the conjurer in the past, regardless of race, authority, or entitlement. The conjurer is a self-ruler and bows before no judge, except the Just Judge, whose badge shines brightest. Judgment and revenge may be the Lord's, but what was carried out for those by the Devil has been shifted to the root man's works. While God has the final say, the root worker makes that path. God says justice comes upon you and the conjurer decides how. Remember, in order for this stuff to not backfire on you or be sent back, it's got to be justified! No matter your situation or the work at hand, keep this in mind when continuing further down this path.

- Take a corn husk and write your name in the center with the twelve names of the disciples surrounding it (Matthew, John, Peter, Andrew, James, Phillip, Bartholomew, Thomas, James, Thaddaeus, Simon the Zealot, and Judas). Go to a graveyard and buy dirt from a baby's grave by exchanging the dirt for three shiny dimes and some candy. Come to and leave the graveyard alone. When buying dirt in a graveyard, keep your head covered and wash the bottoms of your shoes in vinegar before re-entering your home. You're buying dirt from a baby's grave for their innocence. A baby has never been convicted of anything. Place this dirt in the husks and fold it toward you three times, turning it to the right between each fold, and bind it with white thread. Make sure to fold the ends in as well to prevent the dirt from coming out. Carry this with you when going to court by hanging it around your neck with white thread.

- Made candied Chewing John by simmering it in sugar water until most of the water has evaporated. Leave them to dry on a towel. When you head to court, take a few of these pieces with you and pronounce over them, "From roof to ceiling, all tongues speak with me, not against me, as true as every tongue got to confess in the end." Chew the root when you enter the building and be chewing it as you stand before the judge. Chew discreetly, as some courthouses don't allow chewing gum.

- Take some Chewing John, mayapple root, and Queen Elizabeth root (orris root) and bind them together, wrapping toward you, and tie with a red string. Soak them in whiskey overnight while the moon is in the heart (Leo). Dry them out and powder them with a mixture of black pepper and dirt from a baby's grave. Powder it while praying Psalm 5 three times:

  1 Give ear to my words, O Lord, consider my meditation.

  2 Hearken unto the voice of my cry, my King, and my God: for unto thee will I pray.

  3 My voice shalt thou hear in the morning, O Lord; in the morning will I direct my prayer unto thee, and will look up.

  4 For thou art not a God that hath pleasure in wickedness: neither shall evil dwell with thee.

  5 The foolish shall not stand in thy sight: thou hatest all workers of iniquity.

  6 Thou shalt destroy them that speak leasing: the Lord will abhor the bloody and deceitful man.

7 But as for me, I will come into thy house in the multitude of thy mercy: and in thy fear will I worship toward thy holy temple.

8 Lead me, O Lord, in thy righteousness because of mine enemies; make thy way straight before my face.

9 For there is no faithfulness in their mouth; their inward part is very wickedness; their throat is an open sepulchre; they flatter with their tongue.

10 Destroy thou them, O God; let them fall by their own counsels; cast them out in the multitude of their transgressions; for they have rebelled against thee.

11 But let all those that put their trust in thee rejoice: let them ever shout for joy, because thou defendest them: let them also that love thy name be joyful in thee.

12 For thou, Lord, wilt bless the righteous; with favour wilt thou compass him as with a shield.

Do this every morning for three days before the court date.

- Take a purple taper candle and carve your name on one side and "Judge" on the other. Anoint the candle with blessed oil (see page 86). Rub sugar into your name and black mustard into the other name. Set out a glass of water for the spirits. Set the candle on a clean plate by letting the wax drip in the center, then fix the bottom of the candle to it to hold it. Put a tiny dab of Vicks VapoRub on your left ring finger and anoint the outer edges of the plate. Pray that the candle lights the way for justice (make sure you're in the right or that there's a way out), that the sugar sweetens you up, and that the black mustard dissuades the judge from having any adverse thoughts about you. Pray Psalm 5 seven times (see page 139) while the candle burns as the sun goes down. Burn it in increments each day for three days, so the candle finishes the day before your court date.

- As you approach the courthouse, rest your dominant foot on the first step going up and say, "May the Lord bless this house, from the floor to the ceiling. May my word be above all those within, and their words be under my foot."

- Carry these words on paper: "Jesus Nazarenus, Rex Judearum." On the way to the courthouse, recite the following three times, ending the third time with the names of the Trinity:

  I, [name], appear before the house of the judge.

  Three dead men look out the window; one having no tongue,

  the other having no lungs, and the third sick, blind, and dumb.

BRING THE COURT AND JURY AGAINST AN OPPONENT

I assume none of us are blind to the fixed system in some places where bad people get a slap on the wrist or justice isn't properly served. These cases can cause a lot of distress—especially if the person being tried is a murderer or something of that sort. Mind you, when we got caught up in the modern judicial system, we didn't hand over every course of justice. Behind closed doors and drawn blinds, folks would take the spirit of the court into their own hands to bring the law down on a deserving soul. Here are a few ways that's done:

- Take a new bottle bought for this purpose and fill it halfway with apple cider vinegar over the person's name, photo, or foot track. Add a pinch of snuff, a tablespoon of alum, and a table-spoon of guinea pepper. Add thirteen nails one by one, insert-ing them headfirst and naming each one for the judge and jury: "I name thee the judge of the court"; "juror number one, juror number two, juror number three," and so on. Once all of this is done, spit in the bottle while calling the law and court down on their head. Pray that lies fall short in the room and their true nature be shown. Cap the bottle. If the cap is a cork, seal it with wax. If it is plastic, melt the cap with a lighter so it won't be able to be taken off. Every day up until court and until it is completed, shake the bottle three times a day while praying the person will be caught up and justice served.

- Make a mixture of snuff, salt, and alum. Take the person's photo and fold the mixture into the photo, folding away from you, then bind it with a blue string. Place this in a bottle of vinegar and bury it upside down where they'll walk over it or pass by it.

- Gathering the person's foot track works best for this next trick, but you can also take their photo or a paper with their name on it. Burn the paper to ash or take their footprint and mix it with dirt from a police station, a courthouse, and a crossroads. Place this in a jar of vinegar and bury it upside down at a cross-roads as close to the center of town as you can get. This will turn the court on them, but it can also be used to get the police to catch up to someone.

CONJURE BAG FOR COURT

In the event that you go to court and need protection, this hex bag may help. Cut a 4-inch by 4-inch square from the bottom of your right sock (unwashed, of course). In the center, place new salt, High John the Conqueror root, Chewing John, cinnamon, and jack-in-the-pulpit root. Bless these by praying Isaiah 42:5–7 three times over them:

> 5 *Thus saith God the Lord, he that created the heavens, and stretched them out; he that spread forth the earth, and that which cometh out of it; he that giveth breath unto the people upon it, and spirit to them that walk therein:*
>
> 6 *I the Lord have called thee in righteousness, and will hold thine hand, and will keep thee, and give thee for a covenant of the people, for a light of the Gentiles;*
>
> 7 *To open the blind eyes, to bring out the prisoners from the prison, and them that sit in darkness out of the prison house.*

End by saying your name three times.

Tie up the fabric and smoke it with tobacco or incense smoke, calling the four winds to give it breath. Use a candle flame to heat up or cook the root. Then baptize it in your name with water, making the sign of the cross. Call it to wake up. Then give it a name. This is what you will call it by. Carry this with you close to your skin for the first week. Afterward, carry it in your left pocket when going to court. As always, never let anyone touch it and never let it hit the ground.

Worrying about the law and making a living one way or another just to survive takes a lot of energy, but it ain't all just for the comfort of a home and good food on the table. It makes other aspects of life worth it, worth fighting to protect: love. An empty house with nothing but food isn't something most care to come home to. But that special someone, or the want for them, is enough to move mountains.

9

MOCKINGBIRD, MOCKINGBIRD

Back in the day, young'uns dreamed of finding their future spouse, of building a house on a hill in the woods, and living a happy life. For some there were many choices and possibilities in the young bucks and does in town. But how should one know? How could one see what will be? Love is a fundamental thing to our culture. It takes two to make it and two to break it, so if you want it, you need to want it hard for it to last. No amount of magic can create a lifetime's worth of love between you and your lover; that's your job. But who hasn't been in love with the idea of forever love before? Below are some superstitions and tells about future marriages and spouses, including how you can see them in apparitions, visions, dreams, and through divination.

- If you meet someone you know but don't recognize them at first, it's a sign they will be married soon.

- Pick a fresh apple from a tree and hold the stem in your teeth. Turn the apple to the left and on each turn say a letter of the alphabet. The letter at which the stem releases is the first initial of your future love.

- On a day when the sun shines while it is raining, pick up a brick or large stone. You may find a hair from the head of your future spouse to tell what color their hair will be.

- At night on a full moon, step out and look at the first star you see while saying, "Star light, star bright, first star I see tonight, wish I may, wish I might, have this wish I wish tonight." Then reach behind you to pick up a handful of dirt. In it, you'll find a hair from your future lover's head.

- When you first catch a glimpse of the new moon (waxing crescent), step back three steps while saying: "New moon, new moon, come with me and tell me, Who is my true love to be?" Then reach down and grab a handful of dirt, never taking your eyes off the moon. Again, you'll find a hair.

- Make a wish on the full moon, then look under your right foot. If you find a hair, wrap it in a napkin or in the knot of a hankie and sleep with it under your pillow to see your future lover in your dreams.

- Take a lightwood knot (knot of pine) and burn it outside to ash. Then search the ashes for the hair of your sweetheart.

- If you find a bobby pin pointed toward you, carry it with you and someone will ask you out on a date.

- If you are trying to decide what the heart wants, take a bobby pin and have someone name each prong secretly to themselves for both of your potential lovers. Once done, turn down one prong and have your friend reveal what you've done. For example, "You turned down James for John."

- Carry a bobby pin in your shoe all day to dream of your future love that night.

- If your eyebrows meet, you'll marry near home.

- Place an eyelash on your forehead and begin saying the ABCs. The letter the eyelash falls on is the first initial of your intended.

- The first man or woman you shake hands with after kissing a baby will be your future spouse.

- Dreaming of a funeral predicts a wedding.

- If, while doing something, you unknowingly look at the space between your fingers, it predicts a wedding.

- Take a gold ring, preferably your mother's wedding ring. Hang it from a strand of your hair over a glass of water. Each time it strikes the glass, that number is correlated to the letter of the alphabet that predicts your love's name, or their initials.

- Do the same as above, but this time just say the person's name. If the ring strikes two, you'll wear a hole in your shoe (from running after someone who doesn't feel the same). If the ring strikes three, the love is meant to be. If the ring strikes four, they're out the door (nothing will come of it). If the ring strikes five, love will thrive (not necessarily in romance or marriage, though).

- In a room of only women or only men, the first one a cat looks at after cleaning itself will be the first to marry. A variation is to have all participants hold a side or corner of a stretched-out quilt. The cat is then tossed into the center; it will run toward the next to marry.

FINDING OR COMPELLING LOVE

While we can see and divine so far as it comes to future love, we can also draw the attention of lovers as well. In using these charms and methods, you are openly drawing sweethearts to you. You might have one or five knocking on your door!

- Cut your nails every morning on Friday for nine weeks, nine Fridays in total. At the end of this period, your sweetheart will have appeared. If you wish to keep him or her around, soak all those nail trimmings in wine or sweet tea for three days. Strain it and have them drink it.

• To have one love you, take the nail trimming of your left index finger and three hairs from your head, and wet them with a drop of blood from your left little finger if you're a woman, and from the left thumb if you're a man. Tie these in a garment you have worn that hasn't been washed, and bury it in the northeast corner of your sweetheart's property or where they will walk over it frequently. They will dream of you and think of you always.

• Place their photo faceup in a small tin box filled with sugar. Hide this in your chest of drawers and cover with your undergarments. This will sweeten them to you in a less coercive way.

• To have them desire you, gather their foot track from toe to heel and place it under your bed, sewed up in your worn sock, preferably from your dominant side.

• Count nine of their steps. Take dirt from the track of their left heel on the ninth step. If on concrete, just wipe the heel part in a circular position toward you like you're turning a doorknob. Carry this in your pocket or pocketbook for nine days and they'll be crazy for you. Once you've got them, bury the track in the backyard so they'll stay.

• Sew salt into your sweetheart's left pocket without them knowing and they'll never leave your side. Sew it every month on the full moon, especially after sex.

• Take two pieces of paper: one with your name on it, the other with your love's. Dab a bit of molasses on the face of each and glue them together. Bury this on the east side of a willow tree under some moss. You'll fall in love.

- Take heart-shaped leaves and dry them. Crush them into a powder while pronouncing your sweetheart's name, telling them you're all they need and want, that they will have eyes for only you. Sprinkle this over their left shoulder without their knowledge and they'll love you. Repeat every full moon.

- Grated orange candy, sugar, and peppermint make a good old love powder. Sprinkle it over their food without them knowing.

- To have someone fall in love with you, find a pair of mating dogs and throw a piece of clothing over them while in the act. Then wipe your sweat on the clothing and give it to your lover.

- Make a hex bag containing a lock of your hair cut on a Sunday, the peel and seeds of an apple you bit into on a Friday, cinnamon, tobacco, and Adam's needle flowers. Once blessed and awoken, wear the bag around your neck, out of sight. This will attract the attention and desire of potential suitors.

- Twigs from a mockingbird's nest can be used to stir their morning coffee. Then put a drop of your blood in it as well. If you're a woman, the blood must come from the left pinky. For a man, the left thumb. This will surely gain their love, but it must be repeated every month to keep them under.

- If you have an idea of the one you wish to love you, write their name on a piece of brown paper three times in parallel lines. Turn it to the right and write your name over it three times in parallel lines as well. Seal this with a drop of blood. Anoint a white taper candle with olive oil, over which Ruth 1:16–17 has been recited seven times:

  > *16 Intreat me not to leave thee, or to return from following after thee: for whither thou goest, I will go; and where thou lodgest, I will lodge: thy people shall be my people, and thy God my God:*

17 Where thou diest, will I die, and there will I be bur-
ied: the Lord do so to me, and more also, if ought but
death part thee and me.

Roll the candle in cinnamon, nutmeg, and sugar. Make sure not to coat it too much—just enough for a tint and a smell to the wax. Wad the paper up toward you and jab it into the bottom of the candle holder. Place the taper candle on top, and light it while praying the Lord's Prayer (see page 86). Speak to the candle as if it is your sweetheart, telling them to come you to and think of you always, that they won't find rest or be filled in eating until they come to you. Burn the candle every day as the sun rises or as the hand of the clock goes up. When the candle is close to finishing, if they still haven't come to you, "run" the candle by preparing a second one in the same manner and lighting it from the first before it goes out. Continue this until you see results. When results come, keep burning until you're certain they love you; then bury all the wax in the back-yard wrapped in silver foil.

• One of the best times to start any kind of love working or even harvest herbs for love works is when "the air is pink and purple, or orange," as my family phrased it. The orange glow happens a lot at sunrise or sunset in the summer, and the pink happens in the winter. While it's not convenient for some works, you can still boil sugar water while reading the Book of Ruth during these times for added potency, especially if the moon happens to be in the heart (Leo).

WORKS FOR FIDELITY

Remember that Christian taboos were very heavy back in the day here. Women couldn't wear hats or pants to church, only their bonnets.

Divorce was unheard of, but cheating wasn't. It wasn't tolerated, but it happened.

To make a lover be true, take his or her worn left sock and moisten it with black molasses. Roll the sock toward you, starting at the toe, until it's completely rolled up. Now roll it toward you eight more times while telling your lover to stay home and quit messing around with other folks. Take a new red string and wrap the sock by holding a bit of the string under the rolled sock and curving the string up and around toward you. Then wrap the sock in brown paper and place it under your mattress in the center. As the moon grows each month, take it out and spit on it to dress and feed it.

TO TIE DOWN A LOVER'S NATURE

Tying down a man or woman's nature (sexual potency) was the next best thing in getting them to only stay with you and quit with the other lovers they've been seeing. Back in that day, they were bound by their wedding vows. Nowadays, most folks aren't waiting until they're married before having sex—but these works still have power. A piece of advice: If your lover isn't willing to work on your relationship without a root being put on them, then they aren't worth your time! However, love is complex, and every situation and couple is different, so I encourage you to use your own judgment. A friend's husband got tricked by a woman down in Louisiana this way when he was cheating. He said he couldn't leave the house without crying out of shame anytime he went to meet someone. It was so bad, he indeed stopped.

TO TIE UP A MAN'S NATURE:

- Take his semen without him knowing and put it on a red string. Tie five knots in it while reciting his vows to you. If you aren't married, give a command like, "I won't stand for you running around with others, and neither will your member." Say this for every knot. This makes it so that no matter how turned on he may get, he doesn't show any signs of it physically, except with you. It's better if this is done while the moon is in the loins (Scorpio), when they're most vulnerable. Wear this string tied around your dominant ankle.

- Get his semen on a new white bandanna. Take a piece of paper and write his name five times in parallel lines, then turn it to the right and write your name five times over his in parallel lines. It should look like a pound sign of sorts when you're done. Scorch the corners of the paper, put a dab of molasses in the middle, and roll or fold it toward you. Fold the bandanna into a large triangle pointed at you. Then fold the base of this triangle toward you until it makes a strip about an inch or so wide. Place the paper in the middle and tie it up. Keep tying knots into the bandanna, either five or seven in total. It should look like a ball with two little flaps on each side. Powder it with High John the Conqueror powder or powdered ginseng root and hide it in the mattress on his side. If you don't stay or live together, bury it under your doorstep where he'll walk over it, or hang a swag over the door and hide the conjure ball inside so he'll pass under it and be charmed. If you can't sneak a bit of his fluids for this work, take some beard shavings.

To tie up a woman's nature:
- Put a lock of her hair into a dirty sock from your right foot. Then fill the sock with sugar, cinnamon, and powdered peppermint candies. Feed the sock with snail water while calling

her name and telling her to stay put.[2] Tell her this snail water will stick her to you like a briar until you pull her off or let her go. Roll the rest of the sock toward you and sew it shut, sewing toward yourself. Place this in a brown paper bag and hide it in the mattress. Make sure the toe of the sock points inward, not outward from the root. Feed it with your urine monthly and on every important anniversary.

- Take some of her unwashed underwear and tie five knots in it. Powder it with baby powder and place it in a tin can filled with water and molasses. Place a lid on it and bury it beneath the front doorstep or someplace she'll walk over it.

- Take a lock of her hair, some thread from an Adam's needle, and your photo. Roll the photo around the hair and thread and tie it with a red string. Make three knots in the string while calling her name and telling her to stay with you. Hang this above the door or up somewhere she will walk under it.

RELEASE ONE'S NATURE

There comes a time when you might no longer be happy with that certain someone you have tied up. The best and rightful thing to do is to return their nature to them. If this doesn't happen, it can create dangerous situations for both of you. They won't be able to find release unless it's through you, so you will become their target for happiness, for everything they can find with someone else after you've broken it

---

2 Snail water is the juice naturally made by snails and slugs as they move. Snail water is sticky and very hard to remove, which is why it's used to keep something with you. To make a batch, collect twenty cotton swabs of the juice and place them in a jar with 3 tablespoons water and 1 tablespoon salt. Do this during the full moon after a good rain, ideally in April. Steep for a month before using. You can leave the swabs in or take them out after that.

off. I've seen this work take turns into stalking situations and even domestic violence or suicide. You won't want that. So if it comes to that or if they have stopped running around and you feel it's time, you need to release their nature.

- If their nature has been tied up by placing something in the mattress, in the yard, or over the door, take it down and dissemble it. Bury the herb ingredients in separate places in the backyard. For other things that were included, burn them and scatter the ashes at a crossroads.

- If anything had been done with knots in clothing, undo them and burn the garment.

- If the item placed is gone, it will have to be reversed by other means. If it is a man, he needs to take a silver dime (minted prior to 1964) anointed with blessed olive oil. This should then be rubbed outward on his member nine times every day for nine days. Afterward, hand him some snuff soaked in vinegar. Have him smell it and cast it away with the dime at a crossroads. For a woman, she needs to collect her menses on a separate cloth each day for seven days, burning each cloth each day as the sun sets. On the eighth day, the ashes of all these are scattered into a creek or river.

- If this type of work has been done on you and you don't know where the root is, on a Monday take a red string and coat it with your fluids. Powder the string with baby powder and sulfur, then string a silver dime on it in the name of the Trinity. State: "One has come against me and tied me up. I'm all in knots from that one. But there are three who will untie me and I will be free on the Lord's day." Wear it for one week, and on Sunday the bind will be broken.

- If the previous method doesn't work, then you need to take back your nature from the source! Meet with the person whom you suspect has tied you up. Ask them to hold a white hankie or other cloth for a second, one that has previously been moistened with your fluids. As you do that, quietly say, "Tip top, I'll be strong; saddle the rag and we'll be gone!" (The "we" here is you and your nature.) When they hand the cloth back to you, they are unknowingly giving you your nature back.

LOVER RETURN

There are many tales of hearts scorned by a lover leaving, or planning to leave. Oftentimes, the family is hurting and left to fight for themselves. While times have changed, love hasn't. It is still the same ol' sticky mess it was from the get-go with Adam and Eve. Our people courted in the hills at midsummer, swimming in deep blue pools in the mountains, watching fireflies and counting stars before city light blotted them out. Who wouldn't fall in love in a setting like that? Some folks, though, just get so caught up in love they feel they can't live without their spouse or partner when they leave. Below are a few methods to bring a lover back home.

- Take an old pair of their shoes and go to the front porch. Lay one shoe down toe pointing away from the house and the other pointing toward the house. Stand and face the direction they left in and say, "By God, you went away, but by the help of God this will bring you home. I want you to come back to me." Call out their name. Leave the shoes there for nine days, each day going out and saying the same, calling out for them.

- Take their left shoe or an old unwashed left sock and bury it under the porch. Stand in the yard with your back to the house, facing whichever way they went, and call out their name. Do this for nine mornings.

- Whisper their name upon rising and going to bed every day for nine days. On the tenth day, sprinkle salt into the fireplace or on the stove eye while saying, "It is not salt I aim to burn, but my lover's heart to turn. Wishing him neither joy nor sleep, till he come home to me and speak."

- Take three twigs from a mockingbird's nest, and tie a paper with their name or a photo of them to the sticks, facing inward. You can also use hair, if needed. Hang this over the door or in a swag.

- Take a piece of paper with their name written on it three times, crossed with the words "Come back to me" and signed with your signature. Cut the top off a sweet red onion and carve a deep cross in it. Stuff the paper into this cut. Place the onion in a tin can and fill it with molasses and whiskey. Place it under the bed, and talk to it as if it were him every morning until he comes back. "Johnny, come back to me. Turn away from everything and come home."

Family was and is of great importance in the mountains, and although it didn't always consist of blood relation, that blood was a special connection—a continuation and extension of one's own blood, reared and formed to one's own understanding and stories, furthering the patchwork quilt of our ancestors that compose us. One's beloved ones always had priority over all else, spiritually and physically. But the greatest thing beyond finding and keeping love was the fruit it bore and the certainty of the future. The next generation was prayed for, conjured up, blessed, and bathed in the dreams of the family in a day where infant mortality was big and family time was little. Only by God and those with the Gift could call up a soul to be born during the narrowest of windows offered in their old-time mountain lives.

10

LITTLE RABBIT SKIN

Appalachian folk magic recipes are largely tempered by the microcultures they arise from. Just two generations ago in my area in east Tennessee, sex or kids before marriage was unheard of. So was divorce. This mimics the old children's rhyme, "First comes love, then comes marriage, here comes _____ with a baby carriage." While it is preferred for most that a child be born from love, that isn't always the case. However, after the old rhyme, fertility and children are next on our list after love and lust in the life of the old mountaineers. Many families back in the day had huge families with as many as twenty children, either by one woman or many. The average minimum was usually four to six children. Because of this, there are many old wives' tales regarding fertility, childbirth, and child rearing, whether it's how to get pregnant, stop having stillborn babies, ease teething, or weaning a child.

FERTILITY WORKINGS

Everyone is different, of course, and, just like herbal remedies, not everything works for everyone. So some women would resort to different remedies until they found success. Just because something doesn't work for you, though, doesn't mean it won't work for the next person. These works may be used to help you conceive.

- An old work to make a woman fertile involved having a preacher hand the husband or father a can of chickpeas. These were cast onto a busy road and, as they were ground into the mud by traffic, would bring fertility. If you can't find a preacher to help, bury a can of chickpeas at a church for a month, ideally when a blessed day such as Easter or Christmas comes and goes. Then cast the chickpeas into the busy road.

- Boil chickpeas (you can do this after getting them from the church yard as well) as the sun rises while praying Psalm 113:9:

  > *He maketh the barren woman to keep house, and to be a joyful mother of children. Praise ye the Lord.*

- Boil chickpeas in spring water until a third of the water has boiled off. Strain the chickpeas out and bathe in this water for three days. Then sew the dried chickpeas into the mattress you wish to conceive on.

- Rub powdered milk on the skin side of a rabbit hide. Dust this with baby powder and place seven apple seeds in the center with a ginger root. Eat the apple first. Tie the hide into a bundle and baptize it by dunking it in fresh running water in the three highest names. Let it dry in a secluded place, then hide it under the bed. Back in the day, folks would sew something like this up in the head of the bed. This reminded me of a lullaby my grandmother used to sing to us called "Be-oh-bye-oh Baby," which talked about the daddy going hunting to "catch a little rabbit skin to put the be-oh-bye-oh baby in."

- If you wish to have a child, have a friend sit their newborn on your bed or leave a dirty diaper at your house when they leave.

- Eat juicy fruits, such as watermelons, apples, or pumpkins—but nothing acidic, like oranges. For twins, eat twinned fruits.

- Carry a rabbit's foot dressed in rose water and baby powder. Pray Genesis 25:21 over the foot twenty-one times, substituting "Isaac" with the man's name and "Rebekah" with your own name:

  > And [Isaac] intreated the Lord for his wife, because she was barren: and the Lord was intreated of him, and [Rebekah] his wife conceived.

- Make a hex bag of jack-in-the-pulpit root, pumpkin seeds, and a bit of bear's-bed. Wrap these up as the moon grows and lay the bag under the bed when attempting at the most fertile time of the month. As the moon grows, so will your chances of conceiving.

- Another old-timer trick was to acquire butter from a woman named Mary whose husband's name was Joseph, or from a woman whose last name didn't change in marriage (meaning she married an unrelated man of the same surname). Eat a little bit of the butter each day, starting as the moon begins to grow, until you become pregnant. Alternatively, acquire a piece of fabric from such a woman and sew it into a piece of your clothing. Wear this piece until you are pregnant. After the baby is born, cut out the cloth and use it as the baby's first swaddle.

- Sleep with an oblong, phallic-looking stone under your pillow on the night of the full moon and you'll allegedly be pregnant within nine months.

JUMPING DOWN THE BABE

The following tricks, almost entirely based on sympathetic magic, are done to ease labor pains, stop hemorrhage, protect the mother from spirits while giving birth, and ensure safety of both mother and child.

- A knife or axe is placed beneath the bed the woman lies on and a pocketknife or arrowhead is placed under the pillows to cut the pain down. I've seen this work firsthand. Some folks say she should wear the father's hat as well to help with the pains.

- A Bible is placed, open to the Book of Matthew, on the mother's chest if she is in danger and on the mother's belly if the child is at risk in the birthing process.

- It was said that in order to bring on labor, the mother had to walk in circles until she was exhausted.

- Roots and charms were likewise employed next to physical activities such as sex, induced sneezing, or driving over railroad tracks to bring the child. One such recipe calls for tying asafoetida around the neck and placing a rabbit's foot under the bed.

- To induce labor, the father's shoes are placed on the mother's feet while he says, "I gave you this burden and here I relieve you of it." In other areas, the verbal charm isn't mentioned and the father's shoes are worn for strength.

- If the birth is proving difficult, burning corncobs on the porch is recommended.

- Snakeskin was also bound to the woman's thigh for a fast delivery, the basis seemingly being the child will slide right out like a snake.

- Or sew a rattlesnake rattle into a bag and place it in the woman's hand for a smooth delivery. The mother isn't allowed to know what it contains and likewise is barred from opening it to view the contents.

- To help bring the child through, a holey stone (a stone with a natural hole through it) was hung from the rafters of the old cabins back then, right over the mother's head.

- To keep the baby from getting caught up, every open vessel was turned upside down and all knots untied. Additionally, it was recommended that all jewelry be removed from the house altogether. This was usually placed in a small bag or something on the porch until the child came. This not only helped "pour" the child out but also kept the child from getting tangled in the umbilical cord, which was buried in the yard (along with the placenta) afterward with salt. Or, if they wanted more children, the father would carry it over the same number of ridges as children they wished to bear.

STILLBORN BABIES AND MISCARRIAGES

Infant mortality used to be around 50 percent in days gone by. Thankfully, that number has gone down. But it still occurs, whether due to chance or a medical condition. While I'm not prescribing or guaranteeing anything, I do believe that faith and prayer work; and when put together in a root, your chances are improved. My grandmothers used some of these remedies.

- An old superstition for curing the condition or luck that causes stillborn or early death of infants that usually has no cause is to name the next male child Adam. After him, it's said it will stop.

- When Nana had stillborn children, she waded in the ocean at Myrtle Beach. After that, she had no more complications.

You may also wade in the water while praying Psalm 113:9 (see page 160).

- Tie a bundle of church dirt, baby powder, and dogwood bark around your waist to prevent miscarriage.

- Any and all complications were eased by the mother, secretly pregnant, sitting on the unknowing husband's lap.

- A rabbit's foot is carried to help increase the chances of safe delivery. This may be due to the fact that rabbits have many babies so very often, being able to conceive another litter while still carrying a previous litter. They seem to be experts in this area.

ABORTION

It's hard to believe a section on abortion is here, considering the conservative religious influence in this work. However, what the church doesn't know never hurt them. Sometimes a woman would have sex before marriage and end up pregnant. In fear of her family and others, she would resort to anything to be rid of this burden. By all means, see a doctor for this! That said, you have your beliefs, and I have mine; this is here for historical and educational purposes only.

Physical abortions (no magic involved) were rarely spoken of back in the day and of course were seen as a major sin. I heard they used to tell women that after they died, their aborted babies would scratch their eyes out. Physical abortions were done with a large number of things, none of which are recommended, including alcohol, saltpeter, black pepper, turpentine, castor oil, and more. When a procedure could not be done for fear of being caught, women looked to the spiritual roots that abound in these hills.

- An old tale says a woman who wishes to get rid of her child should go to the oldest grave in a cemetery before sunrise. She was to kneel behind the gravestone facing east. As the sun rose, the shadow of the headstone would pass over her belly and take the child with it.

- A red yarn was moistened with turpentine and worn around the waist for nine days to cause abortion.

- It was always said that if a woman continuously carried a pack of salt, it would cause miscarriage. Having a tooth pulled during pregnancy was believed to cause miscarriage, too.

- When the moon was in the bowels (Virgo), a woman would stand on a tree stump on a high hill and switch the stump with cottonwood branches as the sun set. This was usually repeated every Friday night until her flow came and the child was gone.

- A woman would boil an egg in her urine, naming the egg for the child while praying that it not come. She would then bore a hole into the narrow end of the egg and rub graveyard dirt into it. Next, she'd take the egg to an anthill and leave it there. As the ants consumed the egg, so the woman miscarried.

- Women would also squat over a pot of stewed onions to bring a miscarriage.

PREDICT A CHILD'S FUTURE PROFESSION

An old work that was done back in the day, and is still performed now, is to find out a child's future profession. There are of course many variations, but I will only detail a couple here, as the variations are usually minor and only affect the specific items used and the number of them (usually three or five).

A child is sat on the floor facing east before three objects, symbols of their predicted occupation. Whichever one the child grabs or goes to first is the answer for them. Growing up, the items consisted of an empty liquor bottle, a Bible, a piece of wood, a dollar bill, and a bowl of dirt. If the child goes for the liquor bottle, they will be a drunk. If they go for the Bible, they will be a man of God or a churchgoing woman. (If a regular book is used, the child will be very smart.) The piece of wood shows they will work hard for their money, and sometimes predicts a future in carpentry. The dollar bill says they will be wealthy and money will come easily to them, while the bowl of dirt suggests they will be poor all their life. That last one isn't necessarily a bad thing—you can be rich in more ways than with money. Remember, every parent should love their child to death, so this shouldn't have any hinderance on how they are treated or raised. Like with everything, this can change as life goes on.

ENSURE A BABY'S FUTURE SUCCESS

Certain formulas were developed over time to ensure a child's success in life. These methods varied greatly but the majority of them had the child's best interest in mind.

- To ensure book smarts, folks would place a bunch of books under the cradle with the belief that as the child slept over them, they would become more intelligent.

- Arguably, the birthplace of country music is in Appalachia; so it's no wonder so many roots and tales were made surrounding musical talent that could have the potential to "take you to the big city." For this, mothers would rub three living ladybugs on their child's lips or tongue to give them a good singing voice. For musical talent, they would use a cricket.

- To make sure the child will be successful, it was said the child should first be carried upstairs before going down stairs. If the house was just one level, a chair was used to step up on.

- If a mother, while pregnant, becomes interested in an art form, whether music, art, building, or cooking, then the child will be gifted in it.

- Likewise, bodily signs gave an idea of their success: if a baby has long fingers, it suggests musical talent.

- Historically, a baby's first bath should be done when they are four days old in lightly salted water. The salt must be new and bought by an aunt if it's a boy, or by an uncle if it's a girl. If no uncles or aunts are available, parents do it in the same gender respects.

- Make a pouch from the first socks the child wore. On one sock, add a dab of molasses for a sweet life, three quarters for enough money, a pinch of salt for good luck, a piece of bread for abundance, and some church dirt for their angels. Lay the other sock over these and sew them together at the edges. Roll the package up and place it under the baby's cradle. After they are grown enough, this is then placed in a Bible with a lock of their hair at Psalm 23.

- Now having and rearing kids was only half the job done. The other half was making sure they survived. Remember, with no modern medicine, a simple cut on the hand could quickly fester and lead to death. And diseases that we have vaccines for now, such as hives and shingles, were major risks. So, naturally, the second aspect of raising a family was to keep that family healthy. Because without health no work could be done—and you can't survive if you can't make due for yourself. Here is where faith healing and root doctoring come into play.

11

THERE'S A BALM IN GILEAD

No volume on these works would be complete without those recipes that are employed by a large majority of the community—not just the conjurer or preacher. These also far outnumber any other superstition or charm I've ever found.

Since, your health was and is the foundation of your entire life, and even the world of your family in some cases, Appalachian Americans took this power of independence to do things for themselves and try every last resource before requesting help. That independence removed the middle man between man and God and the barrier between religion and superstition. The following are recipes and remedies my family, and many others, have employed for hundreds of years. Remember, this is not a substitute for modern medicine—but it may complement it. And if you're like me and my folks, this is sometimes the only option.

Folk medicine has been well documented in southern Appalachia as well as the South in general, but folk magic has been looked over—which is a shame, as it has connections to every aspect of life in Appalachia, especially when it comes to the health of the family. Prior to the germ theory (and even still today), people believed disease and accidents arise from God, the Devil, haints, or witchcraft. It's no wonder that the resulting diseases of witchery and devilment that befall the body must be met with counter-charms and fervent prayer—especially in the mind of the mountaineer, a mind grown in the wiles of the forever forests, with echoes of angels and demons in an eternal war, with spooks and haints around many corners.

As with every war fought in these hills, we harm ourselves spiritually with whatever works, regardless of what the pastor says about it. Although we are a close, keep-to-our-own-kind culture, deeper within we are a blood-before-water kind of people; family comes first. In this way, folk magic and conjuring lead the way to health and balance in the body. While germs are real and you should definitely wash your hands, spirits can still create imbalances in the body, which lead to illness.

In the infancy of Appalachian folk magic, as our ancestors and the knowledge of their motherlands were slowly mingling over time, medicines were a commonly discussed topic. This occurred all over the South, as new people came with new diseases and native plants were used to help them. Many of my southern readers should be familiar with the phrase "It hurt like the Devil" in reference to a wound or accident. Later, as the belief in magic- and spirit-originated illnesses grew, these became the new "Devil," and thus the phrase "doctoring the devil/root out of you" came about. People would make the root or Devil, and doctor or fix someone with the charm. Following are examples of the former, physical doctoring of the painful Devil.

Note: Before doing any kind of healing for others, you must ask if they have faith in God. Faith is required here. This can even be seen by the actions of Christ: Before he healed the blind man or the lepers, he asked them, "Believe ye that I can do this?" And they all replied with, "Yea, Lord, I do." Faith is required of the soul for the healing of the body and mind.

GENERAL HEALTH

- To ward off disease, a flannel bag containing asafoetida, plus sometimes sawdust and salt, was worn around the neck with the belief that the smell would ward off disease-causing spirits. Much to the same effect, the following character charm, found in *Egyptian Secrets* by Albertus Magnus, is written in white chalk above the front door:

    1. + 2. 7, D. 1. A. + B I 2. S. A. V. + 2 +, H. 6
    f. + B. F. 2, S. + + +

    (The foot of each + should be elongated to form a mini Christian cross. Apply this with all +'s unless specified otherwise.)

- Another recipe for general health calls for the following to be written on brown paper:

    + INTRA + ILLE + CORPUS + CHRISTUS +
    OPUS + INCOLUMIS +

    Place Adam's needle leaves, onion skins, and a dab of honey on top, and fold the paper to make a packet. Bind it with red cord going one way through the square and then the other way. The result should be a red cross on either side.

- Every spring, for general health, go out to a field at midnight on a Saturday and pull the ninth, thirteenth, and twenty-first tuft of grass you find. Cut these up together and brew until ⅓ of the water has been boiled off. Wash with this infused water upward as the sun rises. Toss the remaining wash to the rising sun.

Glory Notes

Another charm often employed was the famous Himmelsbrief (German for "heavenly letter"), known locally as a glory note. They are usually written from the point of view of God, but sometimes consist of a simple written prayer against maladies and danger to the home or family. Those preserved in northern Appalachia usually come with the condition that as long as the bearer follows the commandments and laws of God, they will be protected from all harm, which usually includes illness. However, I have found little evidence for that sort of stance in our glory notes here, likely due to the loose binds of church dogma. Nonetheless, they have a different air about them.

I found one in my grandmother's Bible after she passed; it seems she got it after Papaw passed away, as it is titled "A Prayer for Those Who Live Alone." No author is noted.

> *I live alone, dear Lord*
> *Stay by my side.*
> *In all my daily needs*
> *Be thou my guide.*
> *Grant me good health.*
> *For that, indeed, I pray,*
> *To carry on my work*
> *From day to day.*
> *Keep pure my mind,*
> *My thoughts, my every deed.*
> *Let me be kind, unselfish*
> *In my neighbor's need.*
> *Spare me from fire, from flood,*
> *Malicious tongues*
> *From thieves, from fear,*

And evil ones.
If sickness or
An accident befall,
Then, humbly, Lord, I pray
Hear Thou my call.
And when I'm feeling low,
Or in despair,
Lift up my heart
And help me in my prayer.
I live alone, dear Lord,
Yet have no fear,
Because I feel Your presence ever near.
Amen.

Meant to be recited every so often, its power is still there when it hangs on the wall, rests in a Bible, or sits folded neatly in a wallet.

Here's another example:

In seven days the Lord made the heavens and the earth.
In forty days the earth was washed clean. In one night,
the Lord became flesh. In four days, the dead was raised
by His command. In nine hours He perished and in
three days He pressed the Devil under His heel. The
same do I place under his heel: all witchcraft and mali-
cious tongues, all evil spirits and demons, all disease-
causing spirits and bad winds; under His feet there are
the multitude of the Serpent's babes, crushed beneath the
Name. No fire may lick me, nor flood may wash me; no
lightning strike me or wind cut me; no sun may burn me
nor moon make me made. As truly as Christ hung on
the cross and stepped from the grave.

The above notes may be written down in red ink and hung above the door unfolded, or carried in a poke bag, or simply placed in your purse or wallet. When writing your own glory note, try to relate the actions desired to those of biblical characters. For example, "As Christ knelt in the garden, so too do all malicious spirits bow before the Creator," or "as surely as the three wise men were the first to bow to the Savior, all gun barrels will bow and disarm." These can also be written and then soaked in a glass of water that is then drunk or washed with to effect a cure or result as stated in the note. For added strength, work by the signs: to ward off fire, write the note while the moon is in a water sign; to ward off storms, work while the moon is visible in the sky and is passing through the head (Aries); to ward off illness of the lungs, do so while the sign is in the breasts (Cancer); and for a note against evil spirits or witchcraft, work while the sign is in the bowels (Virgo).

CUTS, WOUNDS, BRUISES, AND SWELLING

To this day, a cut or wound can lead to death, especially if you don't have health care. While it's less likely today, it was common less than four generations ago, when hygiene was poor. In cities like Knoxville and Chattanooga, waste and all kinds of stuff was just dumped right in the street where everyone walked—you can imagine all the diseases and infections that resulted from that.

For cuts and wounds, it was always advised to use the instrument that caused the wound in some way. For a fish hook wound, the fish hook was cleaned well, dried, and then driven into a piece of wood with the belief that as long as it remained clean and didn't rust, the wound would heal quickly; if it did rust, the wound would fester and become inflamed. If you get cut by a knife, the knife is driven into the ground to staunch the blood. If it was a large wound, you'd lay your hand over it while looking at the growing moon while saying, "What I see will increase; what I feel will decrease, in the name of the Father, the Son, and the Holy Spirit."

Here's another: run your hand over the wound, moving away from the heart while reciting,

Wholesome is the wound, wholesome is the hour and sound,
That this may not swell or fester I try,
Until all the seas do run dry.

For bruises, hold your hand on the place and pronounce the following morning, noon, and night for three days:

Bruise, thou shalt not heat.
Bruise, thou shalt not sweat.
Bruise, thou shalt not run,
No more than the Virgin Mary shall
Bring forth another son.

+ + +

To help with swelling, soak tanned eel skin in cheap whiskey for three months. Then rub it on the swelling with the ring and middle fingers, never the dog finger (index finger).

Alternatively, make a bag containing watermelon seeds, pumpkin seeds, and apple seeds, added in that order. Bless the bag by rubbing salt or alum over it while praying for the swelling to decrease. (Don't bless the bag with water, as the swollen body is already retaining water.) You may also recite the previous charm that speaks of increase and decrease, while staring at the growing moon and rubbing the bag. The swelling will decrease just as the size of the fruits decrease from watermelon down to the apple.

CORNS, BURNS, FEVER, AND CRACKING FEET OR HANDS

There are numerous physical and verbal charms used in folk medicine that are too great to show here. However, there are some that are very common because they are often flexible. With a bit of word change, they can be applied to multiple maladies and ailments. The most famous is the first burn charm I was ever taught:

> *Two Angels came from the East*
> *And one from the West;*
> *One brought fire, one brought frost*
> *And the third was the Holy Spirit.*
> *Out with the fire in with the frost.*

Say this three times, blowing on the burn after each recitation but away from the person. With faith, anyone can use this charm.

Here's another charm for healing a burn. Wash the burn with lukewarm water while reciting the following three times in the three highest names, indicated by +++:

> *As Christ was bathed by the River Jordan and made whole,*
> *I bathe the burn with the same for [name] to be whole.*

For cracking feet, folks would use a liniment of some kind, some of which are still available in some places. But the way they'd apply it was the charm: Don't use the dog finger (index finger) when applying the liniment. It's thought that this finger on every human is cursed because that was the finger Judas used to point out Jesus to the guards. Apply it with the middle and ring fingers after a warm bath or shower—but never when it was raining, as this would make the person's feet crack more as the ground dried after the rain.

Fever, a symptom of something greater in the body, was a common cause of death. Because of its nature, it was usually countered with charms much like those used against burns to extinguish the fire in the head. One of the oldest tricks I have found is to wet a rag with cold water and rub it over the head, the back of the neck, and the chest, and down the arms until the rag feels like it's drying. This is the fever getting into the fabric. Take the rag outside and smack it on a tree, rock, or the pavement while telling the fever to leave the person, calling them by name, and stating it cannot return until the Virgin has another child. Finish in the name of the Trinity.

For corns, it was advised to wait for a funeral of someone of the same sex. You don't need to know the person. This was done when the bells of the church tolled, but they don't do that much anymore, so that reference can refer to the bells of "Beulah Land" tolling for the newcomer. Cut out the corns, usually with a pocketknife, and bury them. Then run your fingers over the place and say

> *They are sounding the holy bell and what I now grasp*
> *will soon be well.*
>
> *What ill I grasp do take away, like the dead one in the*
> *grave does lay. + + +*

COUGH, ASTHMA, OR PHLEGM

The charms for respiratory problems are extremely varied. Sometimes they involve carrying a spoken word or physical charm, while other times they consist of odd remedies that have no logical basis behind them. But they may work for some. This category also includes COPD, bronchitis, pneumonia, and other breathing or lung issues.

For pneumonia, the lung of a sheep was placed at the foot of the bed of the sick person and left overnight with the belief that the pneumonia would transfer into the larger "home": the sheep lung. Other folks recommend soaking the feet in whiskey or brandy and then binding onion halves to them overnight. I have done this, and sometimes the onion turned a greenish color from the phlegm being drawn out through the soles.

For general breathing issues, hole a penny that has turned green from oxidation and wear it around your neck so the coin will rest at the center of your chest. This is best done when the moon is in the chest (Cancer). Alternatively, have a person who has never met their father blow into your mouth—or carry a lock of their hair with you.

Here's a charm to be spoken three times while running the hands up the chest and neck, overhead, and to the sky:

> *What has gotten into you? A bad smell or a bad wind?*
>
> *Up and out to hell I send! + + +*

ACHES, PAINS, HEADACHES, AND SPRAINS

In Appalachia, before modern medicine came riding over the hills, our people had their own way of belief in regards to the body, how it came to health or disease. This included simple pains. One belief my family still holds is that pain radiates or "gallops," as Papaw Trivett called it. Many in my family have suffered from fibromyalgia, a disease common among melungeons. The only way I know they bared it was through faith. Nana would speak little of her pain and equate it to the pain Christ felt on the cross. She'd say in passing, "If it didn't hurt him, these pains ain't nothing."

The following charm is along those same lines and can be applied to a number of ailments:

> *They have crucified the Savior on the Holy Cross. It did not hurt him, it did not pain him. Hence, my (thy) sores and sprains will not hurt me (thee). In the name of the Father, the Son, and the Holy Spirit.*

To stop shooting pains, write the following on a piece paper and carry it with you:

ARILL. AT. GOLL. GOTTZO

For sprains, take a long piece of brown paper and soak it in vinegar. Then bind it to the sprain with a piece of red flannel while saying, "Pickle, pickle, make it good, as surely on this earth Christ has stood." This is an example where folk medicine and folk magic or faith mix. We have confidence in both separately, but together they are stronger.

Another for sprains is to rub downward or away from the heart while repeating this charm nine times. (Always mutter your charms, lest others hear you.)

Ronde Geronde

+ + +

Say "prestale" after each interval. Repeat three times for a total recitation of twenty-seven times.

To help alleviate pain, harvest garlic from the garden on Saint John the Baptist's Day (June 24). This was then applied either magically in a carried charm or in a home remedy.

Another charm I recommend often for pain is to get a bowl of foreign dirt, meaning dirt taken far from the person's home or property. (You'll need enough to fill a bowl three times.) Set the bowl on the floor by the person's bed, and each morning their feet should first land on the dirt. Turn over the dirt of their prints with a spoon three times, and toss it out at a crossroads. Do this for three mornings: Wednesday, Thursday, and Friday. This dumps the pain into the dirt.

For headaches, a number of odd things were done. A piece of red flannel lathered with Vicks VapoRub and tied around the head would help. Or tie a red string around the head as the sun goes down and then take the string to an old tree, somewhere folks don't frequent often, and tie it to one of the tree's roots. Then leave it without looking back. (It's better if the ailing person never sees the tree.)

Another is a written charm, a story told using characters from the Bible, that may be carried always:

> *Peter sat on a rock holding his head. Jesus was passing by and asked, "Brother, what aileth thee?"*
>
> *"My Lord, it is the pain in the head that torments me, both waking and sleeping."*
>
> *Christ laid his hand on Peter's head. "No more shall you be pained in the head, nor shall anyone who remembers these words and carries it upon him be pained."*

COLIC AND WHOOPING COUGH

For colic, the following may be written on paper and was usually sewed into the baby's bonnet. Today, you could sew it into the inside of every shirt of the child's, so when the shirt is worn it rests on their breast:

$$S + a + t + t + o + r, A + r + e + p + o +$$
$$T + e + n + e + t, O + p + e + r + a +$$
$$R + o + t + t + a + s^3$$

---

3 According to Albertus Magnus in *Egyptian Secrets*, this charm may also be used to help the mother bear a child easily: Write the charm on a plate and wash it off with wine. Have the mother drink this wine for an easy birth. The charm is placed here because this is the most common usage.

For colic, repeat the following charm three times while running your hand in counterclockwise circles over the baby's belly:

Colic, I embrace thee, I surround thee, I denounce thee,

from this flesh and blood now flee!

Beware thee God, blood and flesh the heavenly host;

Save thee, [name], God the Holy Ghost!

For whooping cough, there are numerous remedies (much like for colic) that straddle the line between medicine and magic. An old-time remedy was to have the child drink water from a vessel that a solid white horse had just used. Another was to pass the child through a blackberry bush where one branch had reached the ground and rooted, creating an arch. The child was to crawl through it three times.

Fabric was also used, with many variations on what kind: a silk ribbon, a leather strap with five knots tied in it, or a strip of black velvet hung around the neck. Alternatively, a bag of asafoetida was worn around the neck.

A "tea" of white ants (termites) was used to cure whooping cough, with the reasoning that if there's something rattling in the chest, the termites would break it down like a log of wood.

Other remedies for whooping cough included drinking stolen milk, having a stallion breathe into the child's mouth, or eating butter kneaded by a woman whose maiden name is the same as her married name.

BLOOD-STOPPING

One of the gifts of the faith healer was the ability to stop the flow of blood, no matter how bad the wound. There are hundreds of stories of how these folks used this gift for their community. Like fire-talking, this was one of the more common gifts used in these hills. Every person had their own way of stopping the blood. Some would hold their hand over the place and go into a trace that ended with speaking in tongues, holy laughter, or treeing the Devil,[4] while others would simply say a verbal charm, usually based on Scripture, while passing their hand over the place. My maternal grandfather was able to do this in person or from a distance via the telephone. He would pass his hand over the place three times—or, if over the phone, he'd hold his hand over the same part that was bleeding on the other person and begin whispering the charm.

Back in the day, a lot of charms could only be taught to the opposite sex and sometimes to only three other people. Papaw taught my mom and Nana some of these charms, which were then passed on to me. However, the famous blood verse (Ezekiel 16:6) has been taught and used so widely, it leads me to believe the following charm isn't held by those folk laws. It is always said three times and finished in the name of the Father, the Son, and the Holy Spirit.

> *And when I passed by thee, and saw thee polluted in thine own blood,*
>
> *I said unto thee when thou wast in thy blood, Live;*
>
> *yea, I said unto thee when thou wast in thy blood, Live.*

When using this next verse, the word *thee* is replaced by the person's name and *he/she*.

---

4 "Treeing the Devil" is an old Baptist practice that comes on when you're in the spirit. Folks would see an evil spirit near, a.k.a the Devil, and they would tree it or chase it off and up a tree, like a hound on a coon hunt. Some healers did this as well in healing diseases, scaring the spirit off with barking and growling mixed with laughter. Today, many see this as a barbaric form of practice and worship, but one of my great-uncles was said to have done this with great success. In healing a person, the Devil is chased around the person, around the house, out the door, and up a tree by the healer, who simultaneously throws handfuls of salt. It is little spoken of or seen anymore, but I'd like to see it revived, as it is an example of the old-time religion of the southern Appalachian hills.

For example,

> *And when I passed by John, and saw him polluted in*
> *his own blood,*
> *I said unto John when he wast in his blood, Live;*
> *yea, I said unto John when he wast in his blood, Live.*

Another for stopping the flow of blood, done in the same manner with the passing of the hand or holding the place if the person is a long distance away:

> *Jesus was born in Bethlehem,*
> *Baptized in the Jordan River.*
> *When the water was wild in the woods,*
> *God spoke and the water stood,*
> *And so shall thy blood.*
> *In the name of the Father, the Son, and the Holy Spirit.*
> *Amen.*

This next one is called Adam's Blood Charm. Pass your hand over the place three times from east to west, reciting the charm with each pass:

> *Through the blood of Adam's sin*
> *Was taken the blood of Christ.*
> *By the same blood I do thee charge*
> *That the blood of [name] run no more at large!*
> *+ + +*

Another:

> *Upon Christ's grave three lilies grow.*
> *The first is named youth;*

The other, Virtue's truth;
The other, SUDUB.
Blood stop.

+ + +

Physical charms were used as well. For a nosebleed, a cold/frozen stone is held to the back of the neck. If you get nosebleeds a lot, a charm stemming from Ireland calls for you to wear a necklace of string with a fishing sinker clamped to it. The string represents the veins and the sinker clamps it to stop the profuse flow of blood. A similar practice among melungeons was to wear a red corn necklace, like that noted by Will Dromgoole in her work *The Malungeons* (1891) when she says an old woman said she had some "blood beads" that were sure to heal many blood ailments. One such necklace has been passed down in my family. For the same, folks would carry a bullet used to kill a hog, or the left hind foot of a rabbit with a black spot on the heel. They'd hold a gold ring on the tongue or a coin to the back of the neck, or they'd wear a bag that contained the Lord's Prayer around their neck.

FIRE-TALKING

Much like blood-stopping, fire-talking, also called blowing out the fire, is one of the most common healing practices in Appalachia. Can you image the danger of an infected burn back in the day? It would've taken no time for gangrene to set in; and if not, no matter where the burn is, it may leave an awful scar. Fire-talking is one of the "miracle magics" our people are known for. There are hundreds of stories of folks getting bad burns that, after the charming is done, heal up fine with no pain and no traces of it left.

Like many gifts, the ones who can do it best are born with the Gift or they gain it through circumstances in life. Papaw Trivett never met his father and was able to talk the fire out of a burn. Any child who has never met their father can do this as well as cure colic and thrash by blowing in the mouth. Unfortunately, Papaw never shared how he did it, so my mother and I can only guess as to the type of charming he used for it. Nana told us about it in passing but never gave any details. A few years after he passed, Mama told me where to look in the Bible, and that's the charm I use now. However, I cannot share it here because it is little known and governed by those same laws. If I shared it, the threat of me losing the Gift could be real, and I wouldn't want that. Instead, I will share others I have learned over the years passed on to me from friends or folks in passing.

The most common physical gesture employed with the following charms is to recite them three times and after each recital you blow on the burn, directing your breath away from the person. Papaw always advised not handling fire on the first day a person's charmed until after sunset, because the fire might jump back in. Folks were of the belief that the fire in a burn would eat away to the bone and set up infection, so when it's talked out you have to wait for the place to close to the flame. It was also sometimes recommended that the burned, after being charmed, should make certain to find themselves indoors come the next sunset or sunrise. Aftercare varied from one healer to the next. Some folks applied unsalted or unwatered butter to the burn on the first day, leaving it uncovered to the breath, and then bandaged it the next day. Others said not to apply anything to it whatsoever, relying on pure faith. In both cases, the burns usually healed quickly with little to no scarring.

Here's one common charm:

> Old clod Clay, Old clod Clay;
> Burn way, burn way.

Another:

> *Bread hunger not. Water thirst not.*
>
> *In the name of the Father, the Son, and the Holy Spirit.*
>
> *Amen.*

And still another, which is more of an exorcism:

> *Wicked flame, I cast thee out of [name] as surely as*
> *Christ stood on the earth.*
>
> *Come out of the marrow and into the bone,*
>
> *Out of the bone and into veins,*
>
> *Out of the veins and into the flesh,*
>
> *Out of the flesh and into the skin.*
>
> *I cast thee out of the skin and into the hair,*
>
> *Out of the hair and into the air.*
>
> *Go where the grass don't grow, and the cocks don't call,*
>
> *And you'll come back none at all.*
>
> + + +

Healing the body by faith is by now a time-honored tradition in Appalachia and is one of the most unique things about us. We've seen how faith handles the ails of the flesh—but what of the soul and spirit?

12

"I'VE BEEN WITCHED!"

The subject of cursing and hexing has historically been filled by the role of the folk witch, the "enemy" you'd least suspect to lay a root under the porch or shoot a witch's gun. Now remember, the conjure folk did this work too, and there was little difference between the two. However, some of the stories we have today are likely exaggerated.

Keep in mind that our folks had their own way about them when it came to God and your fellow man. Everybody's kin. Everybody's welcome. That is, until they prove you wrong. In Appalachian culture, folks will mostly accept you as you are, flaws and all; but we have a couple unspoken laws here: never lie, steal, or cheat. When you think about it, anything someone can do to you or your folks can be summed up in those three things. Murder: they stole a life. Theft, obvious. Gossip, you're lying. Betrayal, you cheated the deal. Keep going: unfaithful lover, back-stabbing friends, folks taking of you without giving back when you need it most. The degrees of what constitutes the need for a curse or hex varies from person to person. Justice is based on the person's individual morals. In Appalachian folk magic, folks went by the biblical "eye for an eye, tooth for a tooth"; however, this doesn't mean you should curse or hex every person who crosses you or gives you the stink eye.

This is here for informational purposes only, and I don't condone hexing or cursing anyone unless you've tried all other avenues without success and it is absolutely necessary. Remember the golden rule: "Do to others as you would have them do to you" (Luke 6:31).

Having a lot of curses under your belt is not something to be proud of or boast about. The true strength of the conjurer is working with both hands: the left hand to make roots and the right hand to break them; however, with this also comes knowing when to throw and when to let it be. When you have a strong connection with your ancestors and spirits, sometimes they take care of things long before you're even able to!

I've cursed a lot of people. That isn't something to be proud of, but I stand by it because I have a stance against certain things like abusive partners, sexual assault, and theft. But regardless of what I think is right or wrong, I will never know both perspectives. Because of this, I always leave enough room for the spirits to enact justice if it is truly needed. Some of my curses have consisted of nothing more than making a doll of a person and setting it upside down on its head in a dark box and forgetting about it, simply letting spirit handle it. Sometimes I will get a little specific as well. But 100 percent of the time, those who have crossed me in awful ways have never found themselves in a better situation.

So before proceeding, keep this in mind: keep a calm heart and never work while you're angry. Anger clouds the mind, and you may do something you'll soon regret. It's a hard job playing the judge when you're the victim, which is to be expected. God says revenge is his, and it's true; but you can still send up your petition. Whatever you get done, God's got as much to do with it as you do.

This is hard work. Curses don't come easy, and you need to be prepared for the consequences. I don't mean karma or anything like that—if the work isn't justified, it can still go through, but if your target is smart enough or spiritual then they can reverse the curse or hex back onto you. You're playing with the scales here, and one wrong move can tip things back onto you. I know this may sound cliché, but "heavy is the hand that bares the root."

A final note: Because of the sour and rotten nature of crossing work, you always need to cleanse yourself afterward, no matter the degree or strength of the work. You don't need that kind of residue clinging to you or just sitting around your home. It'll grow like mold if you let it, slow and unnoticed, but potentially deadly.

STOP GOSSIP

There are many ways to stop the spread of gossip, whether from idol tongues or malicious ones. These recipes all work on the same thing— the tongue—which is why many of the ingredients used are bad tasting, foul, or sour. Anything that draws the face and tongue is used to stop gossip. Because you can't speak while your tongue is tied.

Bottle Work

Take the person's name paper, photo, or another tie you have to them and place it in a bottle of vinegar along with alum, lemon juice, black pepper, and chili pepper. Pray Psalm 5:8–12 over the bottle three times while shaking the bottle every day for nine days:

> 8 Lead me, O Lord, in thy righteousness because of mine enemies; make thy way straight before my face.
>
> 9 For there is no faithfulness in their mouth; their inward part is very wickedness; their throat is an open sepulchre; they flatter with their tongue.
>
> 10 Destroy thou them, O God; let them fall by their own counsels; cast them out in the multitude of their transgressions; for they have rebelled against thee.

> *11 But let all those that put their trust in thee rejoice: let them ever shout for joy, because thou defendest them: let them also that love thy name be joyful in thee.*
>
> *12 For thou, Lord, wilt bless the righteous; with favour wilt thou compass him as with a shield.*

Finish up by rolling the bottle away from you and toward the front door nine times. After the nine days, bury the bottle at a crossroads the person will pass by—or you could keep working the bottle every day until the gossip stops, at which point it may be disposed of.

Alum and Salt Bag

Make up a hex bag containing alum, new salt, black pepper, horsehair, a paper with the name of the gossiper crossed out, and graveyard dirt. Feed the bag with whiskey and bless it over the course of nine days by reciting Psalm 5:8–12 over the bag three times a day:

> *8 Lead me, O Lord, in thy righteousness because of mine enemies; make thy way straight before my face.*
>
> *9 For there is no faithfulness in their mouth; their inward part is very wickedness; their throat is an open sepulchre; they flatter with their tongue.*
>
> *10 Destroy thou them, O God; let them fall by their own counsels; cast them out in the multitude of their transgressions; for they have rebelled against thee.*
>
> *11 But let all those that put their trust in thee rejoice: let them ever shout for joy, because thou defendest them: let them also that love thy name be joyful in thee.*
>
> *12 For thou, Lord, wilt bless the righteous; with favour wilt thou compass him as with a shield.*

On the tenth day, carry the bag with you on the left side of your body. Do this either until you know the talking has stopped or until you lose the bag. If the talking stops and you have the bag, bury it under the roots of a big, secluded tree that doesn't bear fruit.

Powder Recipe

To make a powder to be placed in their tracks, secretly dusted on their clothing or items, or to use in works for the same purpose, take up their left foot track from toe to heel. If you use a paper towel, let it dry and burn it to ash. If it's dirt, use that. Add this to the following mixture: half a cup of cornmeal, a tablespoon of red pepper, a tablespoon of alum, a tablespoon of black pepper, and graveyard dirt. Grind this together using a mortar and pestle. Then add baby powder to help it stick to their shoes. Bless the mixture by reciting Psalm 5:8–12 over it as the sun goes down, three times a day for thirteen days. Remember, when you lay the powder, darken it if need be with some local dirt to help it blend in.

CONQUER ENEMIES

Sometimes you just need an upper hand in overcoming your enemies and their tricks.

* Recite Psalm 44 each day upon waking, at noon, and when you retire.

    1 We have heard with our ears, O God, our fathers have told us, what work thou didst in their days, in the times of old.

    2 How thou didst drive out the heathen with thy hand, and plantedst them; how thou didst afflict the people, and cast them out.

3 *For they got not the land in possession by their own sword, neither did their own arm save them: but thy right hand, and thine arm, and the light of thy countenance, because thou hadst a favour unto them.*

4 *Thou art my King, O God: command deliverances for Jacob.*

5 *Through thee will we push down our enemies: through thy name will we tread them under that rise up against us.*

6 *For I will not trust in my bow, neither shall my sword save me.*

7 *But thou hast saved us from our enemies, and hast put them to shame that hated us.*

8 *In God we boast all the day long, and praise thy name for ever. Selah.*

9 *But thou hast cast off, and put us to shame; and goest not forth with our armies.*

10 *Thou makest us to turn back from the enemy: and they which hate us spoil for themselves.*

11 *Thou hast given us like sheep appointed for meat; and hast scattered us among the heathen.*

12 *Thou sellest thy people for nought, and dost not increase thy wealth by their price.*

13 *Thou makest us a reproach to our neighbours, a scorn and a derision to them that are round about us.*

14 *Thou makest us a byword among the heathen, a shaking of the head among the people.*

15 *My confusion is continually before me, and the shame of my face hath covered me,*

16 *For the voice of him that reproacheth and blasphemeth; by reason of the enemy and avenger.*

17 *All this is come upon us; yet have we not forgotten thee, neither have we dealt falsely in thy covenant.*

18 *Our heart is not turned back, neither have our steps declined from thy way;*

19 *Though thou hast sore broken us in the place of dragons, and covered us with the shadow of death.*

20 *If we have forgotten the name of our God, or stretched out our hands to a strange god;*

21 *Shall not God search this out? for he knoweth the secrets of the heart.*

22 *Yea, for thy sake are we killed all the day long; we are counted as sheep for the slaughter.*

23 *Awake, why sleepest thou, O Lord? arise, cast us not off for ever.*

24 *Wherefore hidest thou thy face, and forgettest our affliction and our oppression?*

25 *For our soul is bowed down to the dust: our belly cleaveth unto the earth.*

26 *Arise for our help, and redeem us for thy mercies' sake.*

- Make a hex bag containing High John the Conqueror root, corn silk, and new salt. Once blessed, feed it with strong whiskey and pray: "As John conquered, so too shall I conquer; as everyone bowed to him, so shall all my enemies bow to me." Finish in the name of the Trinity. Feed it weekly with the same prayer and carry it on the right side of the body or around the neck. As with all charms like this, never let it hit the ground or let anyone else touch it. If no one else even sees it or knows about it, all the better.

- To get the upper hand in the workplace, in wooing a lover, or some similar situation, sprinkle new salt in your shoes.

- Wear the person's picture or name paper facedown in your right shoe until it's worn and illegible. Replace it as needed.

- If you don't know who is coming against you, write on a piece of brown paper "All my enemies" and mark three X's through it. With this make a poke bag containing false daisy, devil's shoestring, and ginseng root. When blessing the bag and praying over it, finish with: "the Devil can't dance when he's kneeling." Wear this bag around your neck and feed it with whiskey.

UPROOT OR HOTFOOT

The term *hotfoot* has been used historically in Appalachia, from Virginia and Tennessee to Kentucky and North Carolina, as well as in the Deep South. Hotfoot means to go very fast or hightail it out of someplace. In *Backwoods Witchcraft* I called it uprooting, because that's what it does. It doesn't matter how long that person has been living in a place—if you work to uproot them, they'll up and go wherever, as long as it's far from you. Here are a few ways to achieve this:

- Take a person's sock or shoe without them knowing, preferably the left one. Sprinkle in some salt, red pepper, and sulfur, then hide the shoe under the porch or somewhere on their property. They'll leave town soon—some say in weeks, others say in nine days.

- Traditional hotfoot powders consisted of mixtures of black pepper and salt; sulfur and salt; salt and graveyard dirt; black pepper and alum; or black pepper and red pepper. This was cast on the person's doorstep or discreetly sprinkled through their home.

- If you can't get near the person's residence or where they frequent before the next rain, you can make a doll of the person and fill the feet with the powder and the heart with any concerns you have of theirs. Bury this at a railroad track with the head pointing out of town or away from your house. If you can't make a doll, place their photo or hair in a jar of powder and shake it for nine days or until they leave while praying Psalm 35:1–6 three times each day over it:

  1 Plead my cause, O Lord, with them that strive with me: fight against them that fight against me.

  2 Take hold of shield and buckler, and stand up for mine help.

  3 Draw out also the spear, and stop the way against them that persecute me: say unto my soul, I am thy salvation.

  4 Let them be confounded and put to shame that seek after my soul: let them be turned back and brought to confusion that devise my hurt.

  5 Let them be as chaff before the wind: and let the angel of the Lord chase them.

  6 Let their way be dark and slippery: and let the angel of the Lord persecute them.

Bury the jar at a crossroads when they leave.

- Take their hair or photo and put it in a snuff box with salt and pepper. Throw this in the river.

- Scatter pieces of lightning-struck wood around their home and under the porch.

SEPARATE LOVERS/CREATE QUARRELS

Separating lovers is one of the areas where justice can be blurred; but workings are usually used to split up your lover and their mister or mistress. Now, there's sometimes a whole emotional can of worms behind folks doing this, which is why I no longer do it for folks—but what you do about a situation is your own business, so here are some recipes to split folks up. These can also be used to simply create fights between two parties, regardless of their relationship with one another.

Cats and Dogs

This method is probably the most popular in all of the South. Take an empty glass bottle (you can reuse a beer bottle with a screw cap—just wash it with vinegar and let it dry for a week or so) and fill it with vinegar. Add black cat hair and black dog hair (both from animals without a speck of white on them), along with the names of both people written on one paper. Mark out all the letters that appear in both names with a slash. This removes the harmony between them. Every day, agitate them by shaking the jar and telling them to fight. Continue until the desired result is achieved, after which the item can be buried at a crossroads.

Moving Candles

Take two white candles and carve the name of one person in one, and the name of the other in the other candle. Anoint them with ditchwater and powder with black pepper. Set them next to each other and light them while praying for the two parties to separate. Move the candles away from each other a couple of inches. Do this each day for nine days as the sun goes down. When they finish, they should be far apart from each other. Dispose of each candle at separate crossroads going different directions.

Boiled Egg to Break Up Parties

Write the names of the two parties on either end of an egg and boil it in water along with 1 tablespoon of vinegar, a bit of graveyard dirt, and some beet juice. Once boiled, peel the egg and burn the shell in a fireplace or pit. Cut the egg in half and feed one to a cat and the other to a dog. The animals should not live in the same home or get along with each other. Alternatively, bury one half near an anthill and the other in a faraway field.

Separation Hex

Make a cloth bundle of bloodroot, beetroot, alum, salt, red pepper, and coal, along with the names or photos of the parties to be separated. Bless the bag and spit on it, cursing the union and praying,

> *A house divided amongst itself cannot stand:*
>
> *so shall you crumble like the temple,*
>
> *so shall you fall like wormwood,*
>
> *so shall you come to ruin like Sodom and Gomorrah.*

Push nine new needles and nine new pins into the bundle and douse it with vinegar. Powder it with asafoetida and bury it on their property where both will walk over it. If it can be concealed under the bed on the boards, that's even better.

MAKE THEM MAD

"Witches" have been causing madness for centuries, just like the conjurer. In many texts of southern footwork, hoodoo, folk magic, and
conjure, there is likely a recipe to cause madness, and it will likely
include a person's hair or underwear as an ingredient. One story I
was told growing up was about a witch named Gussie Proffit who
lived on a mountain outside of a small town in Virginia. She never
caused anyone harm or otherwise aroused any suspicion until the river
flooded and everyone's crops were ruined. The townsfolk blamed the
woman, and a couple men vowed to burn her cabin down, which they
did. Some of it still stood, but she was homeless now with no one but
her pet toad.

A while passed, and those same men decided to go up to her old
cabin and drink their asses off and destroy more things. Then a bad
storm rolled in. Most of them were afraid and wanted to hightail it out
of there, but one man, the presumed ringleader, made them stay and
hold their ground. Once they were calmed down and had returned to
their game of cards, a figure appeared in the doorway. It was the old
woman and in her hand was her toad. A few words were exchanged
between the men and witch. The head man said, "Now you're just
gonna die" and charged after her. Before he could get to her, the toad
jumped and morphed into this great big awful demon creature and
picked up the man by the throat. The other two men, making brown,
ran out of the cabin. Years later, the head man was never the same. He
never came home. Folks would see him wandering the woods following
a toad hopping along, muttering to himself with wide eyes, "I've been
witched. I've been witched." He went mad.

That's what these result in:

- I was always told if you bury someone's hair or unwashed
  undergarments, it will drive them mad.

- Stop their hair up in a bottle filled halfway with water and bury it at the roots of a tree on the north side.

- Place their hair or photo in a snuff box with lye shavings (or limestone) and nine new needles. Toss this in the river to keep their mind wandering.

- Powder the skin of a graveyard snake with graveyard dirt, crossroads dirt, railroad dirt, and white pepper. Scatter this where they'll walk over it.

- Make a doll of the person that includes a personal concern of theirs. Once it is baptized, dip it by its feet into a bucket or cup so it's halfway underwater. Leave it.

- Take a piece of the person's unwashed clothing and use it to make a bundle containing the following: graveyard dirt, mud dauber's nest, corrupted buttercup roots, nine pins, nine needles, nine open safety pins, black cohosh root, white pepper, and two bear's-bed roots that have been tied in an X. Boil this in a pot of water with nine slips of paper, each containing the first portion of Zechariah 12:4:

  > In that day, saith the Lord, I will smite every horse with astonishment, and his rider with madness.

  Recite it until half the water has boiled off. Place it in a good size container and hide it somewhere on the property where they will walk by it. Leave the lid off. As the water evaporates, their mind will go.

TIE UP MONEY

The only time I will ever mess with someone's money or livelihood is when they try to mess with mine. That could be in the form of theft, betrayal, or tarnishing my name or business. The following two recipes are ones I personally use, for individuals or their business. They can not only bring someone down but also shut the doors of the business altogether.

- Borrow a one-dollar bill from the person. On one side, write their name and birthday on all four ends. On the other side, write James 5:1–4:

  1 Go to now, ye rich men, weep and howl for your miseries that shall come upon you.

  2 Your riches are corrupted, and your garments are motheaten.

  3 Your gold and silver is cankered; and the rust of them shall be a witness against you, and shall eat your flesh as it were fire. Ye have heaped treasure together for the last days.

  4 Behold, the hire of the labourers who have reaped down your fields, which is of you kept back by fraud, crieth: and the cries of them which have reaped are entered into the ears of the Lord of sabaoth.

  Fold the bill lengthwise away from you three times to thin their funds. Bind it with a black cord under nine knots. Bury it on their property.

- In a jar place the person's photo and a dime acquired from them. Add devil's shoestring, alum, lemon, corrupted ginseng root, and graveyard dirt.[5] Fill with equal parts beet juice and

---

5 Corrupted roots have been twisted out of form. To corrupt a root such as ginseng, dig the root up yourself and bend it gently without breaking it. While you have it bent, wrap it in string or twine to hold it in place. Let it dry like this. Every day while it dries, rub the root and tell it what it's being remade for. This is done with roots to work the opposite natural effect of them. A "pure" ginseng root can attract strength and luck, while a corrupted one repels it.

vinegar. Every day for thirteen days, roll the jar away from you, toward the doorway, fifteen times while praying James 5:1–4. Do this until the desired result is achieved, then bury it at a railroad track.

The path and work of the conjurer and witchdoctor is one that requires knowledge of two hands. As I said previously, one hand must know how to make up the roots, while the other needs to possess the power to destroy them. Never conjure something you cannot get rid of. As such, let's look at how roots are destroyed and Devils are sent running.

13

RUN, DEVIL, RUN

Now we venture into the realm of the witchdoctor. While the folk healer doctors the Devil out of the body, the witchdoctor doctors the Devils, or roots, out of the mind and spirit. If one is suspected of being cursed or doctored on, there are a few signs that can confirm it. Back in the day, the signs usually consisted of strange feelings or pains shooting through the body, swelling, loss of appetite, nightmares, insomnia, paranoia, and feeling like one is drowning or just an uneasiness about everything. Many folks also find themselves unable to leave their home for long periods of time.

REMOVE HAINTS AND PLAT-EYES

I do not joke when I say you don't know what's out there—what hides behind the lonesome headstone, or why those lights float through the trees in the woods.

In Jonesborough, back in the 1800s, they used public stock posts for minor offenses such as not paying debts owed to the court. The person would be locked in and their ears nailed to the wood and often cut off before being released. For worse crimes, like robbery or horse theft, the Washington County Court would set them to be hung just north of town in a hollow that, due to the frequency of this sentence, came to be known as Hangman's Hollow.[6] Hundreds of folks were hung there. Hundreds left town with little to no ears to speak of. I have not found how many, if any, perished due to infection from their punishments, but I believe we can all take a good guess. Given the grim history of this place, I'd wager there are plenty of haints and plat-eyes lurking about. If you do have a haint or plat-eye, there are many ways to evict them from the property:

- Take a used horseshoe and wrap it in red cloth. Walk around the home from top to bottom, back to front, with all doors open, while holding the horseshoe upside down and saying "Our Father," then reciting Psalm 31:15–17:

  > 15 My times are in thy hand: deliver me from the hand of mine enemies, and from them that persecute me.

  > 16 Make thy face to shine upon thy servant: save me for thy mercies' sake.

  > 17 Let me not be ashamed, O Lord; for I have called upon thee: let the wicked be ashamed, and let them be silent in the grave.

  Repeat this every day for nine days as the sun rises.

- Take the herb false daisy, also called ghost chaser, and cut it up with sulfur, salt, black pepper, and gunpowder. Divide this into four parts and make each part into a hex bag, blessing each by reciting Psalm 31:15–17 three times. Set them in all four corners of the home, except for the last one nearest the front door. Pour a tall glass of whiskey and, with the hex bag, walk

---

6 Back then, a man's horse was the foundation of his livelihood. It enabled him to work for his living or even seek help if needed. Stealing a horse was practically putting a person to death.

from top to bottom, back to front with the whiskey, calling for the spirit to come have a drink. Walk out the door and wait a bit before placing the hex bag next to it. Lead the spirit to the nearest crossroads and walk around in a big circle seven times. This will confuse it. Pour the whiskey out in the center of the crossroads and quickly walk back home without looking back. Keep the hex bags in their place, feeding them monthly with camphor oil or camphor chest rub.

• Hang or carry a hex bag consisting of gunpowder, asafoetida, and sulfur. This will drive the spirit from the home, as they hate the smell it gives off.

• Historically, folks would have a preacher come by and bless the home. They usually did so once a week over a period of time until the house was totally cleaned. They'd go through praying Scripture, anointing doorframes, marking crosses on all mirrors, doors, and windows; they would then verbally plead the blood of Christ against the spirit, praying that the blood cover the home and all those who resided there.

REMOVE EVIL SPIRITS FROM A PERSON, OBJECT, OR PLACE

Psalm 31:15–17 can also be used in the following works. These will remove and purge spirits from a person, item, or place.

• Take some tar water and anoint every wall, window, door, doorframe, and corner with a cross using a horsehair brush. While doing this, say, "Horse find it out, tar send it out." Work from top to bottom, back to front of the home. When you get to the front door, recite Psalm 31:15–17 three times (see page 204). Next, sprinkle cedar, salt, and black pepper through the house for further protection. This may need to be repeated, but if it is successful, then you will hear the house purging itself—creaking or popping sounds, knocks, sounds of things getting knocked off although nothing has moved—which usually last a couple days.

- To chase a spirit from a person, take a bundle of false daisy and whip them with it all over while reciting Psalm 31:15–17. Pat them with the bundle from head to toe, doing three passes in total. Anoint them with olive oil while praying three Our Fathers, then have them stomp on the bushel twenty-one times. Take the bundle outside and burn it to ash, then discard the ashes in a cemetery.

- If the one haunting has left some physical item behind that may be tethering them, place it in a hollowed potato and bind it together. Then bury the potato at their grave or a crossroads if the grave site is unknown.

REMOVE CURSES AND HEXES

Making roots is one thing. The tricky part is killing them—especially when they are made by others. Be diligent: crossed conditions will try to hold you back any way they can. Even if you don't have the energy to work it, do it anyway!

- Go to a new grave on which grass has begun to grow. Take a handful of the grass and pay for it with nine pennies. Add this to a hex bag with new salt, baking soda, ant eggs, and black cat hair. Carry this with you until the bag feels grimy, at which point it has taken the poison and should be cast over the left shoulder into running water. Leave without looking back, no matter what you hear or feel. I've had a few clients tell me that when they used the bag I made them and they tossed it, they heard animal sounds or even a voice calling out their name. That's the root dying.

- To break a conjuring, boil milk with nine gold-eye needles. While it boils, sear the milk with a hot iron. Take the needles out and refrigerate them. Take three drinks each day for nine days. Pour whatever is left on the ninth day into the toilet; the person is to relieve themselves on it and send it on its way.

- Spit on the bristles of the house broom: once for the witch who sent the curse and once for each member of the household. Take the broom and sweep downward on the back of the fireplace or front door while praying Psalm 23 three times (see page 66). Hang the broom above the door for nine days and then burn it.

- Add nine new needles to a pot of water, running each safely between the lips first. Boil the water until it's all gone. Do this every afternoon for nine days. Each day use fresh needles, setting the old ones aside in a white handkerchief. On the tenth day, bury the needles at a crossroads.

- Take a cleansing bath as a complement to the above works. An egg cleansing will work as well, but may need to be done three times in a row for a number of days.

- Take the black or big joker from a new deck of cards. On all four edges write "Run, Devil, run" and in the center write "All Devils." Cut the eyes and hands out of the card and burn them. Fold the card away from you, folding into it devil's shoestring root, kudzu root, graveyard dirt from one of your relatives' graves (one who cared deeply for you), borax, and rattlesnake master. Burn the card at a crossroad, lighting it with a match, and while it's burning toss a pinch of borax into the flame and shout, "Run, Devil, run!" Turn back home while grinding your heels into the dirt or ground and leave without turning back, no matter what you hear.

FOR THOSE WITCHED INTO LOVE

A story I was told growing up was called "Cinder Cat." I don't remember every detail, but it talked about slaves on a plantation, and one of them went to a conjure woman who said another worker on a plantation across the way had put a Devil on her old man so he'd love another woman and not her. The conjure woman advised her to take a grapevine and whip the other woman with it to break the spell. Whipping with branches, in the sense of hitting something or whipping a pot of milk, often come by the same cause: the need to break the power of a root.

- If you suspect you have been witched into love, ask the person to hold a rag that has been wetted with blood from your left ring finger pricked from between the middle and last knuckle while you do something, like tie your shoe. When they give it back, bury it under your doorstep with salt, seven hairs from a fox's tail, and sulfur. Feed it by pouring your first urine of the morning over it for a month.

- Take your left unwashed sock and place a silver dime, alum, sulfur, black pepper, and salt inside it. Put the sock under your mattress and sleep on it until you begin to smell the black pepper. Burn the sock and scatter the ashes at three different crossroads.

- Take an uncrossing bath with salt, Adam's needle root, and devil's shoestring for three days as the sun sets. Toss the remaining bathwater to the west of your property each time.

- Wash your feet each night with vinegar, salt, and red pepper in warm water for nine nights. Toss the water to the west of the property each night. After washing, anoint your feet with blessed olive oil, powder them with baby powder, and put on clean socks before retiring.

- If you believe your partner has conjured you in some way regarding your relationship with them, discreetly place a knife under their side of the mattress and cover it with salt and baby powder. This will break their power over you.

IF YOUR MONEY HAS BEEN DOCTORED

Sometimes money goes out as quickly as it came in, or it just begins disappearing. Fewer customers come by, hours get cut, folks get demoted or laid off. This can be a sign your money has been crossed. For such cases:

- Carry a poke bag made with lodestone wrapped up with your hair, devil's shoestring, salt, a dead cricket, and tobacco. Feed it weekly with good whiskey until your money situation improves. Once it does, bury it at a crossroads.

- Take a dollar bill from your wallet and write "INRI" on all four edges. Write your name in the center. On your name place a dab of molasses, a bit of new salt, and devil's shoestring. Fold the bill toward you three times and sew it closed on all sides. Soak it in just boiled water. Wash your hands in this water every day and sprinkle it on your doorstep and wallet.

- Carry ginseng root wrapped in blue flannel, soaked in whiskey and powdered with the ashes of black rooster feathers for twenty-one days. On the twenty-second day, bury it at a crossroads.

- Take a horseshoe and line devil's shoestring roots, black cohosh root, and cornstarch along the shoe. Seal this with wax while reciting Deuteronomy 30:3–9:

> *3 Then the Lord thy God will turn thy captivity, and have compassion upon thee, and will return and gather thee from all the nations, whither the Lord thy God hath scattered thee.*
>
> *4 If any of thine be driven out unto the outmost parts of heaven, from thence will the Lord thy God gather thee, and from thence will he fetch thee:*
>
> *5 And the Lord thy God will bring thee into the land which thy fathers possessed, and thou shalt possess it; and he will do thee good, and multiply thee above thy fathers.*
>
> *6 And the Lord thy God will circumcise thine heart, and the heart of thy seed, to love the Lord thy God with all thine heart, and with all thy soul, that thou mayest live.*
>
> *7 And the Lord thy God will put all these curses upon thine enemies, and on them that hate thee, which persecuted thee.*
>
> *8 And thou shalt return and obey the voice of the Lord, and do all his commandments which I command thee this day.*
>
> *9 And the Lord thy God will make thee plenteous in every work of thine hand, in the fruit of thy body, and in the fruit of thy cattle, and in the fruit of thy land, for*

*good: for the Lord will again rejoice over thee for good,
as he rejoiced over thy fathers.*

Hang the horseshoe above the door inside the home with points up. This will not only kill the root but restore your luck in money as well.

IF YOUR HEALTH IS AFFECTED

If one's health is affected, wash with the water used by a blacksmith to cook iron. Wash as the sun goes down while praying the Lord's Prayer (see page 86). Or carry a flannel bag of sawdust and seven hairs from the cross on a donkey's back until the bag is lost.

More recipes:

- Soak tanned eel skin in whiskey and wash downward with it upon rising each morning.

- Drink water from which a black cat has drunk while resting the feet on a slab of persimmon bark.

- Boil persimmon bark and nine tablespoons of salt at midnight while calling out the suspected enemy's name. Sprinkle this around the home from back to front and wash the doorstep with it, then sprinkle it in the yard from the porch to the road. This makes any root set against you impotent.

- Boil three cups of mullein at midnight until half of the water has been boiled off. To this add a good amount of Red Eye whiskey until the color changes. Wash the walls of the home with it, in downward strokes; mop the floors with it from back to front; and add it to a cleansing bath. It'll kill just about anything.

- Carry a bag of new salt, bloodroot, and Sampson snake-root. Place it under your mattress. Beneath this, under the bed on the floor, place a bowl of saltwater with two lemon halves in it. When the water has evaporated and the lemon dries, toss it all onto the enemy's property or into running water.

FOR MADNESS

There are a few conjure cures for madness when it has been induced due to witchcraft:

- Wear a bag of buttercup flowers around the neck.
- Carry the bone of a turtle.
- Bathe in warm milk and honey when the moon is in the head (Aries).
- Place the person's hair in a box of new salt and give it to them with instructions to never open it.

CONJURE ROOT KILLERS

These particular roots are some of my favorite. They act like conjure weed killers; anything buried or planted on the land they are used on will be killed by these roots.

- Make a large bundle out of an old shirt of yours filled with salt, black pepper, mullein, red pepper, and borax. Bury in the center of the property and pour vinegar on the place while reciting Psalm 83 three times:

    1 Keep not thou silence, O God: hold not thy peace, and be not still, O God.

    2 For, lo, thine enemies make a tumult: and they that hate thee have lifted up the head.

3 They have taken crafty counsel against thy people, and consulted against thy hidden ones.

4 They have said, Come, and let us cut them off from being a nation; that the name of Israel may be no more in remembrance.

5 For they have consulted together with one consent: they are confederate against thee:

6 The tabernacles of Edom, and the Ishmaelites; of Moab, and the Hagarenes;

7 Gebal, and Ammon, and Amalek; the Philistines with the inhabitants of Tyre;

8 Assur also is joined with them: they have holpen the children of Lot. Selah.

9 Do unto them as unto the Midianites; as to Sisera, as to Jabin, at the brook of Kison:

10 Which perished at Endor: they became as dung for the earth.

11 Make their nobles like Oreb, and like Zeeb: yea, all their princes as Zebah, and as Zalmunna:

12 Who said, Let us take to ourselves the houses of God in possession.

13 O my God, make them like a wheel; as the stubble before the wind.

14 As the fire burneth a wood, and as the flame setteth the mountains on fire;

15 So persecute them with thy tempest, and make them afraid with thy storm.

16 Fill their faces with shame; that they may seek thy name, O Lord.

17 Let them be confounded and troubled for ever; yea, let them be put to shame, and perish:

18 That men may know that thou, whose name alone is Jehovah, art the most high over all the earth.

- This will kill anything buried or laid on your property.

- Vinegar and salt poured on a bag or doll found will kill it. It must never be touched. Pick it up with a stick or something and carry it far from the home after pouring vinegar over it.

- Chickens used to be kept in the yards, some under the belief that they scratch up and kill any works out there.

- Sew black rooster feathers into the bristles of a broom and dress it with whiskey and vinegar, then sweep the yard and porch heading outward to the edge of the property. This will kill any roots, especially those using black chicken parts, because the rooster dominates the hen.

- Mix gunpowder, graveyard dirt, powdered skin from a grave-yard snake, and hair from a solid white rabbit. This recipe will incapacitate and kill any root.

REVERSAL WORKS

Reversal is a form of cleansing in which the roots put against you are deflected back onto their maker. In Appalachian conjure justice is the balance of life, and every action warrants an equal reaction. Appalachian workers generally went by the biblical "eye for an eye, tooth for a tooth," meaning whatever punishment you dish out has to fit the crime. Many folks have requested things that I did not see as justified and I refused to do them. An unjustified work will go through; however, it can be reversed back on to you! If it is justified, it can't be reversed. However, remember that justice is subject to the eye of the beholder: what I think is fair punishment may seem diabolical to another, so follow your heart and morals and be wary if your target should have any lick of sense to know what's going on.

Reversal work is different from cursing work because you are not crafting the root; you're simply picking it up and throwing it back at the sender. Of course, the root can also be removed by cleansing—but sometimes folks need to learn their lesson by the hand of their own bitter roots! Here are a few recipes for sending witchcraft back to its maker:

- Make a poke bag containing cornmeal, salt, and tobacco. Urinate on it while cursing their name and telling the root to go into the bag. Bury it at midnight on their property or somewhere they will walk over it. This of course requires you to know who did the original root and where they live.

- To find out the person who threw against you, write the names of all suspects on separate sheets of paper. Roll the papers into wads using mud or clay from your property. Give them time to dry, then put on a pot of water to boil. One by one, drop each wad into the boiling water, calling for the enemy to be revealed as Judas was revealed a traitor in the end. The first paper that breaks free of its earthy prison and rises to the top is the one.

- Take a candle into which you have carved "my enemies" backward from bottom to top so it reads "seimene ym." Now take a knife and cut the tip of the candle flush so it matches the bottom. Carve the bottom like a pencil until you reveal the wick on that end. As you light the bottom of the candle, read Psalm 7 three times:

1 O Lord my God, in thee do I put my trust: save me from all them that persecute me, and deliver me:

2 Lest he tear my soul like a lion, rending it in pieces, while there is none to deliver.

3 O Lord my God, If I have done this; if there be iniquity in my hands;

4 If I have rewarded evil unto him that was at peace with me; (yea, I have delivered him that without cause is mine enemy:)

5 Let the enemy persecute my soul, and take it; yea, let him tread down my life upon the earth, and lay mine honour in the dust. Selah.

6 Arise, O Lord, in thine anger, lift up thyself because of the rage of mine enemies: and awake for me to the judgment that thou hast commanded.

7 So shall the congregation of the people compass thee about: for their sakes therefore return thou on high.

8 The Lord shall judge the people: judge me, O Lord, according to my righteousness, and according to mine integrity that is in me.

9 Oh let the wickedness of the wicked come to an end; but establish the just: for the righteous God trieth the hearts and reins.

10 My defence is of God, which saveth the upright in heart.

11 God judgeth the righteous, and God is angry with the wicked every day.

12 If he turn not, he will whet his sword; he hath bent his bow, and made it ready.

13 He hath also prepared for him the instruments of death; he ordaineth his arrows against the persecutors.

14 Behold, he travaileth with iniquity, and hath conceived mischief, and brought forth falsehood.

15 He made a pit, and digged it, and is fallen into the ditch which he made.

16 His mischief shall return upon his own head, and his violent dealing shall come down upon his own pate.

17 I will praise the Lord according to his righteousness: and will sing praise to the name of the Lord most high.

- Let the candle burn all the way down over the course of three days, lighting it as the hand of the clock goes down or as the sun sets.

- You may also simply take a cleansing bath for nine days in a row at sunset, replacing your prayers with the recitation of Psalm 7:13–17.

- Take a piece of very thin plywood and draw an image of the person who threw at you. Write their name on the back, and write yours above it. Nail the image to a tree with a long nail, but don't nail it all the way in. Over the course of nine days, hammer the nail in a bit more each time, reciting Psalm 7. On the ninth day, when you drive the nail all the way through, spit on the face of the image. Leave it there to rot. You can place the nail wherever on the photo you wish to hurt them back using the root they threw at you.

- Draw a photo of the person on a piece of brown paper. If you don't know their name, write "All my enemies" over the heart of the image. Wad it up and shove it in the middle of a doughy cathead biscuit. Spit on it and work it into the center of the dough. Then take five new sewing needles and stick them into the dough, all points inward toward the center. Bake it on high as the sun goes down until it's black and charred. Wrap that blackened cathead biscuit in silver paper (aluminum foil) and bury it at a crossroads (one you suspect they pass a lot) at midnight while calling out, "You tried to trip me, but I trip you! Fall like Goliath at the heel!" Turn back the way you came and scuff the dirt under your feet, like a bull. Head home without looking back.

- Wear a silver dime minted prior to 1964 in your left shoe. When you lose it, the spell is broken.

- Draw a picture of your enemy, even just a generic drawing of a person if you don't know who it is, on a piece of paper. Take it to a graveyard entrance or a crossroad in a graveyard and dig a hole. Put some broom straws in the hole to act as a bed, then place the photo facedown over the straws. Light fire to the straws without touching the photo and let it consume the picture to ash. Bury it and stomp on the spot three times, then leave without looking back.

The most essential thing to all of these works, especially the very last that we have seen, is faith. Faith and doubt cannot live in the same house, nor can fear be allowed to stand outside the door. If you plan to do this work, you must do it with every bone of your body and have nothing but trust in God and the spirits. You must have a strong will: you'll be conjuring angels and battling Devils to a fuller degree than most have ever witnessed. This is a way of life, and while it isn't for everyone, it is a calling that is a reward in its own. There is of course no need to be a professional at this: most folks work and use some things here and there to simply better the deck that life deals them, and that is fine.

CONCLUSION

The stories of a people keep their culture alive. For a long time, a part of Appalachian culture and history has been missing, left behind by historians and scholars, left in pieces by folklorists who collected data regarding our medicines and superstitions. Until now, this work hasn't been recognized as an actual system, only a compilation of the "ignorant" beliefs we hold. Swept under the rug, placed in the corner, the conjurers and doctors of yore demand to be recognized for their contributions to the life and survival of many communities, especially during times of war and injustice. We don't expect to be understood, but we deserve to have our stories returned to us to carry into the continually progressing world we live in today.

Society is fragile, and we still recognize that here. At any moment, everything we know could come crashing down around us. But we know where we'll be and what we'll do. We'll continue to work with the land, our communities, and the Lord to get by. Thus, we may eventually need to fully return to these old, "barbaric" ways of superstition and magic that our ancestors relied on. So there it is. Revived and alive for another day.

A

ZODIAC SIGNS AND THEIR CORRESPONDING BODY PARTS

Aries: Head, face, ears

Taurus: Throat and neck

Gemini: Arms, shoulders, and hands

Cancer: Chest, breast, sides, and stomach

Leo: Heart and back

Virgo: Digestive system, intestines, colon, and spleen

Libra: Kidneys, lower back, and buttocks

Scorpio: Reproductive system and sexual organs

Sagittarius: Hips, thighs, and liver

Capricorn: Knees; all joints and skeletal system

Aquarius: Ankles, calves, and circulatory system

Pisces: Feet and lymphatic system

SIGNS FOR WORKINGS

Aries: Head, thoughts, dreams, calling someone, make them see something, etc.

Taurus: Stop gossip or draw the truth from someone; musical talent

Gemini: Double the quantity of something; strengthen your reach or influence in a situation

Cancer: Strength, dominance, fertility, success

Leo: Love, emotions, all matters of the heart; dominance, success

Virgo: Cursing/hex work against luck and health; cleansing

Libra: Law and justice work

Scorpio: Fertility and sex/lust; secrecy

Sagittarius: Protection and speed

Capricorn: Dominance, all works on animals

Aquarius: Cleansing, baptism, and working with the dead

Pisces: Foot track magic, removing or setting obstacles in one's path, and strength to stand your ground

B

LIST OF HERBS/CURIOS AND THEIR USES

From here, you will have to have the judgment to know which herbs to use in what manner or for what purpose. The recipes given previously in this book use traditional herbs and items found in these mountains, whether naturally or, historically, in local stores. Each herb or item has its own particular potency for the heading it is under and may be stronger than an herb neighboring it. Every conjurer worked differently in Appalachia. Some folks would use a handful of herbs available to them, while others had storehouses for when they were in need; the whole natural world was the conjurer's toolbox.

While things vary in our tradition from other folk magic systems, the spirit is generally the same. Use what you've got. If you live in these hills, then a lot of the herbs and things below are available to you in the woods or through connections with farmers or hunters. Substituting one herb for another listed here is fine, but be mindful of its potency. Fresh herbs used and allowed to dry in hex bags may be stronger for you than starting out with a dried herb. Just like with the witching sticks and the bones, the roots will speak to you. What they require or what power they give to one conjurer oftentimes isn't the same for another. For example, you might feel that High John the Conqueror root is stronger that ginseng; but to another, ginseng might feel stronger. So listen to everything.

This is a large list, but it is far from complete. The flora and fauna of Appalachia are almost endless and surely abundant! There are many things used in regions that vary greatly from those used in, say, just a county or two over. Listed here are those (usually) easily accessible to you, whether in grocery stores or roadside ditches. Some may even be growing in your backyard already!

PROTECTION FROM CONJURING AND UNNNATURAL ILLNESS

Use these items to repel jinxes, hexes, and the evil eye; keep off haints; and protect against witchcraft, accidents, and lightning.

- Adam's needle and thread (leaves and roots)
- Ammonia
- Angelica root
- Ant eggs
- Anthill dirt
- Asafoetida
- Baby powder
- Balm of Gilead (buds and bark)
- Basil
- Bear's-bed
- Beet (root and juice)
- Bermuda grass
- Black beans
- Black cat fur

- Black chickens (rooster or hen, eggs, feathers, dried feet)
- Black cohosh root/black snakeroot
- Black cow milk
- Black dog hair
- Black pepper
- Boneset
- Borax (20 Mule Team)
- Bullets (spent)
- Burnt/scorched cotton
- Button snakeroot/rattlesnake master
- Candles burned during Christmas dinner
- Candle from a funeral
- Cast iron
- Cat's-claw root
- Chamomile
- Christmas fern
- Clover (hop/red/white/four-leafed)
- Deer's eye root/ black-eyed Susan root
- Devil's bit
- Devil's shoestring
- Devil's-walking-stick (thorns and roots)
- Dimes (silver, minted prior to 1964)
- Ditch dirt
- Ditchwater
- False daisy/ghost chaser

- Fern, male
- Five-finger grass/cinquefoil
- Foxtail fur
- Frostroot/Poor Robin's plantain
- Garlic
- Ginger root
- Ginseng root
- Morning glory root
- Goat milk or goat hair
- Grapevine (leaves and bark)
- Graveyard dirt
- Gunpowder
- High John the Conqueror root
- Holly
- Holy water
- Horehound
- Horsehair
- Horsetail grass
- Hyssop
- Indian Head pennies (worn, carried, or nailed face out over the front door)
- Iron
- Lemon juice
- Lime Juice
- Limestone

- Lye (soap)
- Maidenhair fern
- Master of the woods/woodruff
- Masterwort/master root
- Mica
- Mistletoe
- Myrrh resin or incense
- Pawpaw (leaves, roots, seeds)
- Plantain
- Pleurisy root
- Purslane
- Rattlesnake fern
- Red Eye liquor (hot and spicy liquors)
- Red pepper
- Rhubarb
- Rosemary
- Salt (table, epsom, ice cream, or canning)
- Saltpeter
- Snakeskin
- Solomon's seal root
- Star anise
- Sulfur
- Vinegar
- Virginia creeper
- Virginia snakeroot

- Well water
- Whiskey
- White mustard seeds
- Witches'-butter (fungus)

CLEANSE AND PURIFY

- Alum
- Ammonia
- Apples
- Baby powder
- Black cow's milk
- Bluing
- Boneset
- Borax
- Bouncing bet/lady's washbowl
- Camphor
- Cedar
- Chicken/turkey feet (borrowed from the Deep South)
- Church dirt, grass, leaves
- Dimes (minted before 1964)
- Dogwood (leaves and branches)
- Eggs
- Elderberry
- Epsom salts
- Five-finger grass/cinquefoil

- Flannel
- Grapevine (leaves and bark)
- Hyssop
- Iodine water
- Iron
- Joe-pye weed/queen of the meadow (stalks)
- Kudzu
- Lemon
- Lime
- Pine (needles, bark, and resin)
- Pine-Sol
- Poke (leaves, harvested in early spring)
- Red Eye liquor
- Salt
- Saltpeter
- Tar water (pine tar soaked in water)
- Water (spring, creek, well)

KEEP THIEVES AND UNWANTED PEOPLE AWAY

- Adam's needle and thread (roots)
- Ammonia
- Angleworm powder
- Ant eggs
- Anthill dirt

- Bear's-bed
- Black cat fur
- Black chicken feathers
- Black pepper
- Christmas fern
- Church dirt
- Deerskin
- Deer's eye root/ black-eyed Susan root
- Dirty dishwater
- Ditchwater/ditch dirt
- Doodlebug dirt
- Elderberry bark
- Fern, male
- Morning glory root
- Grapevine (leaves and bark)
- Hen and chickens (plant)
- Lemon
- Lime
- Limestone
- Lye
- Magnolia (bark)
- Maidenhair fern
- Mica
- Pawpaw (leaves, roots, seeds)

- Plantain
- Rattlesnake rattle
- Red Eye liquor
- Red Pepper
- Salt
- Saltpeter
- Snakeskins
- Tobacco
- Witches'-butter (fungus)

SAFE TRAVEL OVER LAND OR WATER

- Anthill dirt
- Apple seeds
- Black pepper
- Chewing John (galangal root)
- Church dirt
- Dimes (minted before 1964)
- Feverfew
- Five-finger grass/cinquefoil
- Graveyard dirt
- Meadowsweet
- Mugwort
- Red brick dust
- Red pepper

- Salt
- Saltpeter
- Yarrow

WARD OFF NIGHTMARES

- Adam's needle and thread (threads from the leaves)
- Apple seeds
- Asafoetida
- Baby powder
- Bear's-bed
- Bermuda grass
- Bible
- Black pepper
- Cattail seeds
- Christmas fern
- Church dirt
- Coffee
- Coral
- Dandelion leaves and flowers
- Elderberry bark
- Eel skin (tanned leather)
- False daisy/ghost chaser
- Five-finger grass/cinquefoil
- Frostroot/Poor Robin's plantain

- Garlic
- Grapevine (leaves)
- Graveyard dirt
- Gunpowder
- Kudzu leaves
- Lavender (flowers and roots)
- Mugwort
- Plantain
- Rattlesnake fern
- Rattlesnake rattle
- Red brick dust
- Red pepper
- Ripple grass/Bullhorn plantain
- Salt
- Saltpeter
- Water from a creek running east
- White mustard seeds
- Yarrow

RETURN ROOTS TO SENDER

- Angleworm powder
- Ant eggs
- Anthill dirt
- Asafoetida

- Bear fat
- Beef tallow
- Blackberry roots
- Black chicken (feathers and eggs)
- Black pepper
- Cat's-claw root
- Cattail root
- Chewing John (galangal root)
- Church dirt
- Crawfish (powdered)
- Devil's shoestring
- Devil's-walking-stick
- Ditchwater
- Foxtail fur
- Ginseng root
- Grapevine (bark and vines)
- Graveyard dirt
- High John the Conqueror root
- Hobblebush root
- Horsehair
- Lemon
- Lime
- Limestone
- Low John (trillium)
- Lye

- Minnows
- Pleurisy root
- Railroad dirt
- Rattlesnake fern
- Rattlesnake skin
- Red Eye liquor
- Red pepper
- Salt
- Sulfur
- Tobacco

BREAK CURSES, JINXES, HEXES

- Adam's needle and thread (roots)
- Angleworm powder
- Ant eggs
- Asafoetida
- Baking soda
- Bear's-bed
- Black cat fur
- Black pepper
- Black rooster feathers
- Bloodroot
- Borax
- Butter (made on Christmas, Good Friday, Easter)
- Butterfly weed/pleurisy root

- Button snakeroot/rattlesnake master
- Candle burned during Christmas dinner
- Christmas fern
- Devil's shoestring
- Dogwood bark
- Five-finger grass/cinquefoil
- Foxtail fur
- Foxtail grass
- Frankincense
- Ginseng root
- Grapevine (bark and vines)
- Graveyard dirt
- Great bulrush
- Hyssop
- Joe-pye weed/queen of the meadow
- Kudzu
- Morning glory root
- Mountain mint
- Oak
- Pawpaw (leaves, roots, seeds)
- Red brick dust
- Red pepper
- Salt
- Saltpeter
- Sampson snakeroot

- Silver
- Slippery elm
- Solomon's seal root
- Stinging nettle
- Sulfur
- Sweet gum (bark, leaves, balls)
- Tobacco
- Witches'-butter (fungus)
- Whiskey

CURSE, CROSS, HEX, OR WITCH

- Adam's needle and thread (leaves and thread; roots)
- Asafoetida
- Beet (root and juice)
- Blackberry (fruits, leaves, root)
- Black chicken eggs or feathers
- Black mustard seeds
- Blueberry (fruit and leaves)
- Bittersweet
- Chicory root
- Coal
- Coffee
- Devil's dipstick (fungus)
- Devil's shoestring
- Devil's-walking-stick (thorns)

- Grapevine (bark and vines)
- Graveyard dirt
- High John the Conqueror root
- Jezebel root (Louisiana iris root)
- Kudzu root
- Lichen (from graveyard or north side of tree)
- Lightning-struck wood
- Madder root
- Mud dauber's nest
- Needles and pins
- Pawpaw (leaves, roots, seeds)
- Red Eye liquor
- Red pepper
- Salt
- Snakeskin
- Sulfur
- Tobacco
- Vinegar
- Walnut
- Witches'-butter (fungus)

HOME BLESSINGS, PEACE AND JOY

- Apple (bark, flowers, fruit, seeds)
- Basil
- Beetroot

- Bloodroot
- Bluets
- Cattail seeds
- Corn (silk and flower)
- Corn roots
- Dandelion root
- Deer's eye root/black-eyed Susan root
- Deerskin
- Ginseng root
- Green bean root
- Lavender
- Lemon
- Lime
- Limestone
- Loadstone
- Low John (trillium)
- Madder root
- Mica
- Morning glory root
- Red brick dust
- Red onion skins
- Rhododendron (flowers, bought from the plant with the shiniest dime)
- Rhubarb root
- Rose

- Rosemary
- Salt (new)
- Sourwood (leaves and bark)

KEEP THE LAW AWAY

- Angleworm powder
- Anthill dirt
- Asafoetida
- Bear fat
- Bear's-bed
- Black mustard seeds
- Caraway seeds
- Cattail root
- Chewing John (galangal root)
- Christmas fern
- Cinnamon
- Clove
- Coal
- Corncobs, dried
- Deer's eye root/black-eyed Susan root
- Foxtail fur
- Grapevine (leaves and bark)
- Graveyard dirt
- Honeysuckle
- Indian Head pennies

- Jack-in-the-pulpit
- Kudzu
- Lightning-struck wood
- Madder root
- Nutmeg
- Pawpaw (leaves, roots, seeds)
- Pumpkin seeds
- Rabbit Foot
- Red Brick Dust
- Reindeer moss
- Tobacco
- Vinegar
- White clover
- White oak (bark)
- Witches'-butter (fungus)
- Yarrow

FOR COURT CASES

- Black mustard seeds
- Buckeye
- Calendula
- Chewing John (galangal root)
- Deer's eye root/black-eyed Susan root
- Ginseng root
- Goldenseal root

- Lightning-struck wood
- Morning glory root
- Mud dauber's nest
- Pumpkin seeds
- Red pepper
- Sweeteners (sugar, syrup, molasses)
- Vinegar
- Yarrow

ATTRACT MONEY, GOOD LUCK, AND SUCCESS

- Alfalfa
- Allspice
- Alum
- Arrowhead, large leaf
- Arrowroot
- Beans
- Biscuits (catheads)
- Black cat hair
- Bluing
- Buckeye
- Calendula
- Chicken breast bone
- Cinnamon
- Clover (red, white, four-leaf)

- Coal
- Coffee
- Collards
- Copper pennies
- Cornmeal
- Corn silk/cobs
- Deer's eye root/black-eyed Susan root
- Devil's shoestring root
- Figs
- Five-finger grass/cinquefoil
- Flour
- Galax (leaves)
- Ginger root
- Ginseng root
- High John the Conqueror root
- Honeysuckle (leaves and flowers)
- Huckleberry
- Job's tears
- Limestone
- Loadstone
- Morning glory root
- Mud dauber's nest
- Mulberry
- Nutmeg
- Pawpaw (leaves)

- Rabbit foot or skin
- Raccoon skin/penis bone
- Sassafras (root and bark)
- Sweeteners (sugar, syrup, molasses)
- Tobacco
- Whiskey
- Wish bone
- Witches'-butter (fungus)

GET A JOB OR PROMOTION; GAIN FAVORS

- Arrowhead, large leaf
- Arrowroot
- Bear's-bed
- Blue-eyed grass
- Buckeye
- Chicken breast bone
- Christmas fern
- Church dirt
- Coffee
- Galax (roots)
- Limestone
- Loadstone
- Master of the woods/woodruff
- Mulberry

- Railroad dirt
- Salt

DRAW CUSTOMERS

- Alfalfa
- Allspice
- Ammonia
- Buckeye
- Cinnamon
- Coffee
- Five-finger grass/cinquefoil
- Galax (roots)
- Ginger root
- Ginseng root
- Gunpowder
- Honeysuckle (roots)
- Limestone
- Loadstone
- Mud dauber's nest
- Red brick dust
- Reindeer moss
- Sassafras root and bark
- Sweeteners
- Tobacco
- Witches'-butter (fungus)
- Yellow dock root

FOR LUCK IN GAMBLING AND GAMES OF CHANCE

* Arrowroot
* Aster flowers
* Black cat bone
* Black cat fur
* Blue-eyed grass
* Bluets
* Buckeye
* Chestnut
* Hickory
* Honeysuckle flowers
* Jerusalem star (flowers)
* Pawpaw (leaves, roots, seeds)
* Pool chalk
* Red onion
* Reindeer moss
* Salt
* Tobacco
* Whiskey
* Witches'-butter (fungus)

LOVE, LUST, MARRIAGE, FIDELITY

* Adam and Eve root/puttyroot
* Adam's needle and thread (flowers)

- Angelica root
- Angleworm powder
- Apple seeds and skins
- Balm of Gilead buds
- Bachelor's buttons/cornflowers
- Bloodroot
- Blowball/dandelion
- Bluebells/Virginia cowslip
- Candy (peppermint and hard orange)
- Calamus root/ sweet flag
- Catnip
- Chestnut
- Cherry (bark and fruit)
- Chickweed
- Cinnamon
- Coffee
- Deerskin
- Five-finger grass/cinquefoil
- Galax (leaves)
- Ginger root
- Ginseng root
- Grapevine (leaves and bark)
- High John the Conqueror root
- Honeysuckle (root, leaves, flowers)
- Johnny-jump-up/wild pansy

- Lavender
- Licorice root
- Loadstone
- Mace/nutmeg
- Mimosa tree (pods and flowers)
- Mockingbird nest pieces
- Morning glory flowers
- Myrtle
- Oranges
- Paper birch bark
- Queen Elizabeth root (orris root)
- Rabbit skin or foot
- Raccoon penis bone
- Raspberry
- Red clover
- Red onion
- Rhododendron
- Rhubarb
- Rose
- Rosemary
- Sampson snakeroot
- Senna
- Low John (trillium)
- Sweeteners (sugar, syrup, molasses)
- Sweet potato roots and flowers (taken up at the strike of heat lightning)

- Tobacco
- Whiskey
- Wine
- Yarrow
- Yellow dock root

FIDELITY; TO QUIT RUNNING AROUND WITH OTHER LOVERS

- Adam's needle and thread (flowers)
- Angleworm powder
- Anthill dirt
- Button snakeroot/rattlesnake master
- Chestnut
- Comfrey
- Cow droop (dirt from paths made by cattle in hillside)
- Dove feathers
- Grapevine (leaves and bark)
- Kudzu (vines and leaves)
- Loadstone
- Magnolia (leaves, flowers, and seeds)
- Mimosa (flowers)
- Mockingbird nest pieces
- Mud dauber's nest
- Paper birch bark
- Red onion

- Senna
- Snail shells (powdered)
- Snail water (trail from a snail)
- Snakeskin
- Sweeteners (sugar, syrup, molasses)
- Sweet potato roots and flowers (taken up at the strike of heat lightning)
- Tobacco
- Whiskey
- Wine
- Witches'-butter (fungus)
- Vinegar
- Yarrow
- Yellow dock root

HAVE A LOVER RETURN

- Angleworm powder
- Anthill dirt
- Balm of Gilead buds
- Bear's-bed
- Black cat hair
- Bluebells/Virginia cowslip
- Chestnut
- Christmas fern
- Deer's eye root/black-eyed Susan root

- Fern, male

- Ginger root

- Ginseng root

- Goldenrod

- Goldenseal

- Honeysuckle

- Joe-pye weed/queen of the meadow

- Johnny-jump-up

- Kudzu

- Limestone

- Loadstone

- Madder root

- Nutmeg

- Peach

- Queen Anne's lace root

- Queen Elizabeth root/(orris root)

- Red onion

- Salt

- Tobacco

- Vinegar

- Whiskey

BREAK UP LOVERS

- Alum

- Ammonia

- Asafoetida
- Beet (root and juice)
- Black cat hair
- Black chicken eggs and feathers
- Black dog hair
- Black pepper
- Bloodroot
- Chestnut hull (sharp outer cover)
- Coal
- Garlic
- Ginger root
- Jezebel root (Louisiana iris)
- Kudzu root
- Lemon
- Lime
- Madder root
- Maidenhair fern
- Mud dauber nest
- Pawpaw (leaves, fruit, roots)
- Red Eye liquor
- Red pepper
- Salt
- Stinging nettle
- Sulfur
- Tobacco

- Vinegar
- Whiskey

FERTILITY

- Apple
- Bear's-bed
- Christmas fern
- Cross
- Dandelion root
- Deer's eye root/black-eyed Susan root and flower
- Eggs (preferably the first eggs a hen has ever laid)
- Foxtail grass
- Ginger root
- Ginseng root
- Honeysuckle
- Jack-in-the-pulpit
- Kudzu
- Lavender
- Lovage/bo' hog root
- Molasses
- Peach
- Pear
- Pine
- Pumpkin seeds
- Queen Elizabeth root (orris root)

- Rose
- Tobacco
- Watermelon

DIVINATION AND SPIRIT CONJURING

- Apple seeds
- Chestnut
- Corn kernels
- Doodlebug dust
- Eggs
- Frankincense
- Joe-pye weed/queen of the meadow
- Magnolia (leaves)
- Myrrh
- Pawpaw (leaves, roots, seeds)
- Peach
- Salt
- Sunflower seeds
- Tobacco
- Red bud tree (buds and bark)
- Walnut tree (leaves and bark)
- Water
- Whiskey
- Witches'-butter (fungus)

PHYSICAL HEALTH

- Adam's needle and thread (thread and leaf points)
- Buckeye
- Buttercups
- Chestnut
- Copper wire
- Honey
- Horehound
- Joe-pye weed/queen of the meadow
- Master of the woods/woodruff
- Nutmeg
- Oats
- Onion
- Pawpaw (leaves)
- Queen Elizabeth root (orris root)
- Red pepper
- Salt
- Sunchokes/Jerusalem artichoke
- Tobacco
- Whiskey
- Witches'-butter (fungus)

MENTAL HEALTH; FOR MADNESS OR INSANITY

- Alum
- Baking soda

- Buttercups
- Cardinal feathers
- Cow droop
- Dandelion (flowers)
- Dogwood
- Elderberry
- Frankincense
- Honey
- Horehound
- Hyssop
- Joe-pye weed/queen of the meadow
- Kudzu root
- Lemon
- Magnolia
- Nutmeg
- Salt
- Tobacco
- Whiskey

BIBLIOGRAPHY

Banker, Mark T. *Appalachians All: East Tennesseans and the Elusive History of an American Region*. Knoxville: University of Tennessee Press, 2011.

Barden, Thomas E., ed. *Virginia Folk Legends*. Charlottesville: University of Virginia Press, 1994.

Battle, Kemp P. *Great American Folklore: Legends, Tales, Ballads, and Superstitions from All Across America*. Garden City, NY: Doubleday, 1986.

Bible, Jean Patterson. *Melungeons Yesterday and Today*. Signal Mountain, TN: Mountain Press, 1975.

Blue Ridge Reading Team. *Stories 'Neath the Roan: Memories of the People of Yancey, Mitchell & Avery Counties at the Foot of the Roan Mountain in North Carolina*. Avery County, NC: The Team. 1993.

Botkin, B. A. *A Treasury of Southern Folklore: Stories, Ballads, Traditions, and Folkways of the People of the South*. New York: Crown Publishers, 1949.

Boyle, Virginia Frazer. *Devil Tales*. New York: Harper & Brothers, 1900.

Bradley, Bob. *This Here's Country: Legends and Folklore from East Tennessee Hill Country*. Bristol: Bradley, 1996.

Brake, Katherine. *How They Shine: Melungeon Characters in the Fiction of Appalachia*. Macon, GA: Mercer University Press, 2001.

Bruchac, Joseph. *Hoop Snakes, Hide Behinds, & Side-Hill Winders: Tall Tales from the Adirondacks*. Freedom, CA: Crossing Press, 1991.

Burdock, Lewis Dayton. *Magic and Husbandry: The Folklore of Agriculture*. Binghamton, NY: Otsiningo Publishing Company, 1905.

Campbell, John. *Witchcraft and Second Sight in the Highlands and Islands of Scotland: Tales and Traditions Collected Entirely from Oral Sources*. Detroit: Sing Tree Press, 1970.

Casetta, Anna, Wayland D. Hand, and Sondra B. Thiederman, eds. *Popular Beliefs and Superstitions: A Compendium of American Folklore.* 3 vols. Boston: G. K. Hall and Company, 1981.

Cavender, Anthony. *Folk Medicine in Appalachia.* Chapel Hill: University of North Carolina Press, 2007.

Cavender, Anthony P., and Donald B. Ball. "Home Cures for Ailing Horses: A Case Study of Nineteenth-Century Vernacular Veterinary Medicine in Tennessee." *Agricultural History* 90, no. 3 (Summer 2016): 311–337.

Chadwell, J. Tyler, and Tiffany D. Martin. "Mountain Mystics: Magic Practitioners in Appalachian Witchlore." *Bulletin of the Transilvania University of Brasov, Series IV: Philology & Cultural Studies* 1 (2016): 49–56.

Cooper, Horton. *North Carolina Mountain Folklore and Miscellany.* Murfreesboro, NC: Johnson Publishing Company, 1972.

Cross, Tom Peete. "Witchcraft in North Carolina," *Studies in Philology* 16, no. 3 (July 1919) 217–287.

Drake, Richard B. *A History of Appalachia.* Lexington: University of Kentucky Press, 2001.

Dromgoole, Will Allen. 1890. "A Strange People." *Nashville Sunday American,* September 15, 1890. *melungeon.org.*

Dromgoole, Will Allen. 1890. "Land of the Melungeons." *Nashville Sunday American,* August 31, 1890. *melungeon.org.*

Dromgoole, Will Allen. 1891. "The Malungeons." *The Arena,* March 1891. *melungeon.org.*

Dromgoole, Will Allen. 1891. "The Melungeon Tree and Its Four Branches." *The Arena,* March 1891. *melungeon.org.*

Duncan, Barbara R. *Living Stories of the Cherokee.* Chapel Hill: University of North Carolina Press, 1998.

Frazer, James. *Folklore in the Old Testament.* New York: Avenel Books, 1988.

Gainer, Patrick. *Witches, Ghosts, and Signs: Folklore of the Southern Appalachians.* Grantsville: Seneca Books, 1975.

Goss, Linda, and Marian E. Barnes, eds. *Talk That Talk: An Anthology of African-American Storytelling.* New York: Simon & Schuster, 1989.

Gunn, John C. *Gunn's Domestic Medicine*. Louisville, KY: Charles Pool, 1838. Available online at *collections.nlm.nih.gov*.

Gutch, Mrs., and Mabel Peacock, eds. *County Folk-Lore Vol. 5, Printed Extracts No. VII, Examples of Printed Folk-Lore Concerning Lincolnshire*. London: David Nutt, 1908.

Guy, Joe. *The Hidden History of East Tennessee*. Charleston, SC: History Press, 2008.

Hahn, Emily. *Breath of God: A Book about Angels, Demons, Familiars, Elementals, and Spirits*. New York: Doubleday, 1971.

Hamilton, Mary. *Kentucky Folktales: Revealing Stories, Truths, and Outright Lies*. Lexington: University Press of Kentucky, 2012.

Hand, Wayland D. "Magical Medicine: An Alternative to 'Alternative Medicine.'" *Western Folklore* 44, no. 3 (July 1985): 240–251.

Harden, John. *The Devil's Tramping Ground and Other North Carolina Mystery Stories*. Chapel Hill: University of North Carolina Press, 1949.

Hicks, Ray. "The Mountain Fortuneteller." *Jack Alive!* June Appal Recordings, compact disc. 1989.

Hohman, John George. *Pow-Wows or Long Lost Friend: A Collection of Mysterious and Invaluable Arts and Remedies, for Man as Well as Animals, with Many Proofs*. Pennsylvania: John George Hohman, 1819.

Hurston, Zora Neal. *Every Tongue Got to Confess: Negro Folk-Tales from the Gulf States*. New York: HarperCollins, 2001.

Hyatt, Harry Middleton. *Hoodoo-Conjuration-Witchcraft-Rootwork*. 5 vols. Hannibal, MO: Western Publishing, 1970.

Jameson, W. C. *Buried Treasures of the Appalachians: Legends of Homestead Caches, Indian Mines and Loot from Civil War Raids*. Little Rock, AR: August House Publishers, 1991.

Jones, Loyal. *Faith & Meaning in the Southern Uplands*. Champaign: University of Illinois Press, 1999.

Lane, Megan. "Hoodoo Heritage: A Brief History of American Folk Religion." master's thesis, University of Georgia, 2008. *lane_megan_e_200805_ma.pdf*.

Magnus, Albertus. *Egyptian Secrets or White and Black Art for Man and Beast*. Chicago: De Laurence, Scott & Co.,1916.

Marshall, Geraldine Ann. *The Homeplace History and Receipt Book: History, Folklore, and Recipes from Life on an Upper Southern Farm a Decade Before the Civil War.* Golden Pond, KY: The Friends of Land Between the Lakes, 2012.

McCallister, Ron. *Frontier Medicine: Practitioners, Practices, and Remedies on America's First Frontier, Northeast Tennessee, 1770–1850.* Piney Flats, TN: Rocky Mount Museum Press, 1999.

Milnes, Gerald. *Signs, Cures, and Witchery: German Appalachian Folklore.* Knoxville: University of Tennessee Press, 2007.

Mooney, James. *The Swimmer Manuscript: Cherokee Sacred Formulas and Medicinal Prescriptions.* Edited by Frans M. Olbrechts. Washington: U.S. G.P.O., 1932.

Mould, Tom. *Choctaw Tales.* Jackson: University Press of Mississippi, 2004.

Ossman & Steel. *The Guide to Health or Household Instructor.* Wiconisco, PA: Ossman & Steel, 1894.

Petro, Pamela. *Sitting Up with the Dead: A Storied Journey Through the American South.* New York: Arcade Publishing, 2001.

Price, Charles Edwin. *Demon in the Woods: Tall Tales and True from East Tennessee.* Johnson City, TN: Overmountain Press, 1992.

Price, Charles Edwin. *Haunted Jonesborough.* Johnson City, TN: Overmountain Press, 1993.

Richard, Chase. *American Folk Tales and Songs.* New York, NY: Dover, 1971.

Rinzler, Carol Ann. *Feed a Cold, Starve a Fever.* New York: Oxford, 1991.

Russel, Randy. *Mountain Ghost Stories and Curious Tales of Western North Carolina.* Winston-Salem, NC: John F. Blair, 1988.

Schwartz, Alvin. *Cross Your Fingers, Spit in Your Hat.* J. B. Lippincott: Philadelphia, 1974.

Sutherland, Herbert Maynor. *Tall Tales of the Devil's Apron.* Johnson City, TN: Overmountain Press, 1988.

Tallman, Marjorie. *Dictionary of American Folklore.* New York: Philosophical Library, 1959.

Teuton, Christopher B. *Cherokee Stories of the Turtle Island Liars' Club.* Chapel Hill: University of North Carolina Press, 2012.

Thacker, Larry. *Mountain Mysteries: The Mystic Traditions of Appalachia.* Johnson City, TN: Overmountain Press, 2007.

Varner, Gary R. *Creatures in the Mists: Little People, Wild Men and Spirit Beings around the World.* New York: Algora, 2007.

Walser, Richard. *North Carolina Legends.* Chapel Hill: University of North Carolina Press, 1980.

Whedbee, Charles. *The Flaming Ship of Ocracoke and Other Tales of the Outer Banks.* Winston-Salem, NC: John F. Blair, 1996.

Wigginton, Eliot. *The Foxfire Book.* 12 vols. New York: Anchor Books, 1977.

Winkler, Wayne. *Beyond the Sunset: The Melungeon Outdoor Drama, 1969–1976.* Macon, GA: Mercer University Press, 2019.

Winkler, Wayne. *Walking Toward the Sunset: The Melungeons of Appalachia.* Macon, GA: Mercer University Press, 2004.

Young, Richard. *Ozark Tall Tales.* Little Rock, AR: August House, 1989.

ALSO BY JAKE RICHARDS

Backwoods Witchcraft: Conjure and Folk Magic from Appalachia

Conjure Cards: Fortune-Telling Card Deck and Guidebook

Ossman & Steel's Classic Household Guide to Appalachian Folk Healing: A Collection of Old Time Remedies, Charms, and Spells

TO OUR READERS